Mental Health Skills for Clergy

Mental Health Skills for Clergy

DANA CHARRY

Clergy

Evaluation/Intervention/Referral

Judson Press ® Valley Forge

Mental Health Skills for the Clergy

Copyright © 1981
Judson Press, Valley Forge, PA 19481

Library of Congress Cataloging in Publication Data

Charry, Dana.
  Mental health skills for clergy.

  Includes bibliographical references and index.
    1. Church work with the mentally ill.   2. Mental
illness. I. Title. [DNLM: 1. Mental disorders.
2. Pastoral care.   WM 61 C485m]
BV4461.C47   253.5   80-27515
ISBN 0-8170-0886-1

The name JUDSON PRESS is registered as a trademark in the U.S. Patent Office.
Printed in the U.S.A. ✛

To my wife, Ellen

Preface

The year 1975 was a turning point in my professional life. At that time, I had recently finished residency and was beginning to pursue a fairly ordinary career in psychiatry. The event which changed this occurred one day when I was invited to join the faculty of a newly established program for training clergy in counseling skills and psychotherapy.

The idea of working with clergy was new, but felt very familiar. As the son of a rabbi, I had grown up in an environment of religious traditions and practices. I had known a clergyman's life from the inside and had a firsthand sense of the number of people who come to the clergy with emotional problems.

My five years as teacher and clinical supervisor with the Pennsylvania Foundation of Pastoral Counseling has proved to me the great importance of psychiatrists and the clergy working together in maintaining mental health. This cooperation, I believe, is one of the expanding frontiers of my profession.

I am grateful to many people whose influence helped to shape this work:

—to my father, who was my first model of a helping professional;

7

—to Dr. James Ewing, who showed me an example of sensitive humanity blended with a keen, clinical skill;

—to Drs. Robert Dow, Roy Lewis, and Patricia Middleton—cofounders of the Pennsylvania Foundation of Pastoral Counseling, colleagues, and friends—who taught me much about teaching and learning;

—and to my students, whose questions and insights have helped to keep these ideas growing.

Dana Charry, M.D.
January, 1980

Contents

Mental Health Skills for Clergy

 ONE

Introduction

In modern-day America, there are many institutions and practitioners who are known as providers of mental health care. These include Community Mental Health Centers, counseling centers, psychiatrists, psychologists, and psychotherapists of every conceivable background and orientation. Yet, when faced with emotional problems, the majority of people do not go directly to these professionals for help. In most instances, a troubled individual turns first to someone who is closer to home, both literally and figuratively—someone who is known, who is easily accessible, and whose judgment and advice can be trusted. In a large number of cases, the one who is first contacted is a clergyperson.

In a study published in 1960[1], a large sample of Americans were asked to whom they turned first when they had emotional problems in the past. The largest group—42 percent of the respondents—stated that they went to a member of the clergy; only 31 percent went directly to a mental health practitioner or agency. The study was repeated in 1976 and the results were similar: 39 percent indicated that they turned first to the clergy for help with emotional problems.[2] The President's Commission on Mental Health, which carried out an extensive survey of mental health care in this country, acknowledged the key role of the clergy in the provision of that care. In its 1978 report, the commission noted that:

> Religious leaders, professional and lay, at any one time are in face-to-face relationships with hundreds of thousands of persons who are in emotionally hazardous periods of stress such as are caused by illness, surgery, accidents, divorce, natural disasters, unemployment, moving, and by many forms of loss and grief.[3]

The clergyperson can be thought of as a "gatekeeper" who stands at the entrance to the mental health care system. Many of the people who consult the clergyperson need not proceed any further and can be adequately helped without any referral. But a significant number will need to be referred, and for these people the clergyperson plays the very important role of a guide and adviser who helps them through the entrance to an unfamiliar land.

This book does not deal with techniques of pastoral counseling or psychotherapy, although an increasing number of clergy are being trained in both of these skills. It is intended, rather, for the clergy who are not trained psychotherapists, but who are faced daily with the problems of troubled people. The aim of this book is to help the clergyperson to be a more effective gatekeeper—to recognize those who will need to be referred, to grasp quickly the nature of their problems, to deal with their immediate crises, and to help them move on to the more specialized help which they need.

The first portion of the book (chapter 2) deals with the general topic of referral, an act which requires considerable skill and sensitivity. Included in this chapter is a discussion of how to make effective use of a psychiatric consultant. The succeeding chapters discuss those individuals who present the clergyperson with particularly difficult problems of crisis intervention and referral. These include the psychotic person (chapter 3), the suicidal person (chapter 4), the seriously depressed person (chapter 5), the drug or alcohol abuser (chapter 6), and the person with brain disease (chapter 7). An additional chapter deals with the subject of psychological factors in physical illness (chapter 8), and the book concludes with a discussion of psychotherapy, a modality of treatment which may be of great benefit to many of the clergyperson's parishioners (chapter 9).

Underlying everything written in this book is the fundamental assumption that clergy and psychiatrists can and should work together as colleagues, with mutual respect for one another's skills and experience. At times in the past, psychiatry has been blemished by an attitude which dismissed the religious dimension of life as simply an "illusion," or at best a neurotic solution to unconscious conflict. Many of the clergy, by the same token, have seemed to assume that all psychiatrists are insensitive, unfeeling individuals with no appreciation for that which is moral, spiritual, or otherwise unscientific. The time is long overdue for the elimination of such narrow thinking on both sides. It is hoped that this book will speed the process of bringing together these two groups of professionals whose good working relationship can bring immeasurable benefit to the troubled people whom we all serve.

 TWO

Referral

The dictionary defines the verb "to refer" as: "to send or direct to some person or place, as for treatment, aid, decision, etc." In this broad sense, referral is not limited to the helping professions; it takes place every day between friends, family members, and co-workers for all manner of services. For our purposes, we will focus on a specific type of referral: that made by a clergyperson to a mental health profession. This subject is the first to be discussed in this book, since it is the foundation and the final common pathway for everything that follows.

Who Should Be Referred?

Individual members of the clergy will vary in personality and counseling skills, and some may have special training in addition to seminary education. For the clergyperson without specialized training, however, the following suggestions will serve as general guidelines.

There are five categories of individuals who should always be referred to a psychiatrist or a psychiatric facility at least for an evaluation, and usually for ongoing treatment as well. The clergyperson may play an important role with these people during their treatment but should not try to counsel these individuals alone. These five groups will be listed and described briefly here; each one is discussed at greater length in subsequent chapters.

The first category of individuals who should be referred consists of those who are psychotic, who are out of touch with reality to a major degree. These are people who show delusional thinking or very inappropriate or bizarre behavior. These people, in most cases, can benefit from medication and may need to be hospitalized. They also require a very specialized form of psychotherapy.

The second group includes those people who are overtly suicidal or who have a history of making suicide attempts in the past. These individuals may also need hospitalization, and their treatment calls for special therapeutic approaches. Treatment of these people also involves ethical and legal responsibilities which the average clergyperson should not be expected to assume.

Third is the group of people with significant problems of drug addiction or alcohol abuse. Medical problems of detoxification and drug withdrawal often arise in the treatment of these people, and they may need to be admitted to a medical hospital or a specialized drug or alcohol treatment program.

In the fourth category of people who should be referred are those who show signs of severe depression which interferes with their physical functioning and their day-to-day activities. These people usually need medication, hospitalization, or other specialized treatment.

The last category includes those people who show signs of brain disease—signs which include confusion, disorientation, and memory loss. Many of these people respond well to medical therapy, and they may need the attention of an internist or neurologist, as well as a psychiatrist.

The majority of people who consult a clergyperson, however, usually do not fall into any of the five categories listed above. The majority are people with problems in living, with anxieties and fears, with mild depression, and with personality traits which get them into difficult situations. With this large group of people there are no hard-and-fast rules as to whom the clergyperson should refer. The decision depends on a number of factors, including the clergyperson's training and competence, available time, and degree of interest in counseling.

It also depends upon whether or not the clergyperson's own personality makes a workable match with the personality of the one who is seeking help. Every counselor and mental health professional discovers through experience that there are certain types of individuals and certain kinds of problem situations in which his or her counseling is consistently effective, and others in which it consistently fails to be of help. This should be no cause for shame or embarrassment since it is simply a reflection of each individual's uniqueness and inevitable limitations. One of the most important skills of counseling is the ability to recognize as early as possible those persons whom one is not able to help, and to refer these people as smoothly and rapidly as possible in the appropriate direction.

To Whom Should the Clergyperson Refer?

The variety of mental health facilities which are available, particularly in large urban centers, can sometimes be confusing. The situation can be simplified if these facilities are divided into four groups: specialized agencies, Community Mental Health Centers, other institutions, and private practitioners.

Specialized Agencies

A specialized agency, as the name implies, offers help for only one type of problem or one particular category of persons. Included here are child-guidance clinics, family counseling services, and marriage counseling centers. This category also includes such services as vocational training and rehabilitation agencies, transitional living facilities, and residential programs for adolescents. Special programs also exist for the treatment of such problems as drug addiction, alcoholism, gambling, and obesity. Each community will have a different array of such agencies, and the clergyperson should become acquainted with each one. A personal visit to such an agency can provide a great deal of useful information and create a channel for future referral.

Community Mental Health Centers

The system of Community Mental Health Centers was established by the federal government in the mid-1960s. The aim of the system was to provide publicly subsidized treatment for the mentally ill, mentally retarded, and emotionally disturbed within their home communities, rather than at large, remote state hospitals, as had been the case in the past. In this sense, the centers have been highly successful, for the population of the state hospitals has been greatly reduced, and most psychiatric treatment today is done on an outpatient basis with only brief hospitalizations required.

Under the Community Mental Health system, each state is divided into areas ("catchment areas") based on geography and population. One catchment area contains between 75,000 and 200,000 people. In each area, one Community Mental Health Center is established, and all those who live in that area can be treated at that center on a sliding fee scale according to income.

In actual practice, the system is still incomplete, and there has not yet been a center established in every area. At the present time, only about half the population of the country is covered by the Community Mental Health system, but new centers continue to be developed every year.

In heavily populated urban centers, the catchment areas are relatively small, and a large city may contain ten to twenty such areas. In sparsely populated regions, on the other hand, a single catchment area may cover as much as a thousand square miles. This difference in size has very real practical significance. For the city dweller, the Community Mental Health Center may be a ten-minute bus ride away, while the rural farmer may have to travel an hour or more by automobile to reach his designated center. But for a large segment of the population of this country, the Community Mental Health system has put mental health care within convenient range, both geographically and financially.

Community Mental Health Centers are set up in such a way that they can deal with a wide variety of emotional and mental problems. Every person coming to the center has a full psychiatric evaluation, and in most cases the center can provide the necessary treatment, either inpatient or outpatient. In those instances where the center cannot provide the treatment, the staff will make a referral to an appropriate agency which can do so.

One of the most important aspects of the Community Mental Health Center is that it is expected to maintain a twenty-four-hour, seven-day-a-week emergency service, with psychiatrists and other professionals available. Here again, the system is not yet fully developed, and not every center has a full round-the-clock service. The clergyperson should investigate the situation in the local center, if one exists. If an emergency service is in operation, its telephone number should be kept readily accessible at all times.

Centers are staffed by a group of professionals with different training, who work together in such a way as to ensure that the best qualified person does the treatment in each case. People who need medication are seen by psychiatrists, and decisions for hospitalization are also made by psychiatrists. Psychotherapy or counseling is usually done by psychologists, social workers, psychiatric nurses, and other trained therapists. The patient does not actually choose the therapist or psychiatrist, but an effort is made to match each patient with staff members who are both qualified and compatible with the patient. If the match turns out to be unworkable, the patient can request a change of staff.

If a Community Mental Health Center exists in the clergyperson's area, it can be an immensely valuable resource. A visit to the local center will enable the clergyperson to see the facility and make personal contact with some of the staff. Such a visit would be welcomed by the center staff, since the clergyperson represents a significant source of referrals. Both parties stand to gain from a good working relationship.

Other Institutions

A variety of general treatment and counseling facilities may also exist, particularly in areas which do not have a Community Mental Health Center. General hospitals often have psychiatric outpatient and/ or inpatient departments, and university hospitals are almost certain to have such departments. Private, free-standing mental health centers also exist in some communities. These are not government-subsidized, in contrast to the Community Mental Health Centers, and usually charge higher fees than the latter. Pastoral Counseling Centers also have sprung up over the past twenty years in many locations.

No blanket statement can be made about all these facilities, and the clergyperson should attempt to investigate every such facility in the local area. This requires an investment of time, but the investment is amply rewarded when a referral is needed.

Private Practitioners

In most communities, one can find mental health professionals who function on a private practice, fee-for-service basis. Psychiatrists, like other physicians, are licensed by the state and can practice either singly or in groups. Most states also allow psychologists and social workers to set up private practices, although specific licensure require-ments may vary from one location to another. In some areas, pastoral counselors and others with degrees in counseling may also practice privately.

There are a number of factors for the clergyperson to consider when deciding whether to refer to a private practitioner or to an insti-tution. Location and accessibility are obviously important to consider. The private practitioner may be personally familiar, while the institution may be unknown and therefore seen as frightening. In dealing with private practitioners, a person can choose the professional whom he or she prefers, and the practitioner may have more convenient office hours than the institution. On the other hand, private practitioners' services are usually more expensive than those of an institution, and not all private practitioners are covered by health insurance plans. Furthermore, many private practitioners may not be available in an emergency, whereas the Community Mental Health Center or the local hospital usually is.

For people who fall into one of the five categories listed in the first section of the chapter, the most appropriate private practitioner is a psychiatrist. As a medical doctor, a psychiatrist can prescribe medi-cation, has access to a hospital if necessary, and can assess organic brain disease and physical illness. The psychiatrist also has specific training in dealing with psychotic and suicidal individuals. For those who do not fall into one of the five categories, a referral to a psychiatrist can still be made, but this is not essential. These people can be given good treatment by trained nonmedical psychotherapists. (See chapter 9 for further discussion of psychotherapy.)

One of the most important ingredients in a successful referral is the clergyperson's own acquaintance with the practitioner to whom he or she is referring. As with agencies and Community Mental Health Centers, the clergyperson should make personal contact with several practitioners in the community and ideally should pay each one a personal visit. The best approach to take in such a visit is one of honesty and frankness. The clergyperson should not hesitate to ask the practi-tioner about such things as the nature of his or her practice (general or specialized), fees, office hours, or the general type of therapy which the practitioner does. Such a discussion can lead to a relationship of understanding, trust, and mutual respect, which is the best foundation for a successful referral in the future.

With these practical considerations in mind, we can now turn to a consideration of the dynamics and techniques of referral.

The Referral Process

Referral is not an isolated act; it is a process which requires time, skill, and sensitivity. Accomplishing a successful referral can be almost as complicated as doing good psychotherapy, and in light of this it is surprising that the subject is given only very brief attention in most textbooks and training programs.

Referral is difficult to accomplish because it calls for a significant shift in thinking, by both the clergyperson and the parishioner.

(For the sake of simplicity, the term "parishioner" will be used to denote the person being referred. In practice, the person may not always be a member of the clergyperson's congregation.)

The parishioner, first of all, has chosen to come to the clergyperson rather than to a mental health professional. In most cases, his or her expectation is that the clergyperson will be able to provide whatever help he or she needs. The referral requires that the parishioner give up this expectation and accept the idea of going to another person for help.

For the clergyperson, the act of referral demands the recognition and admission of limitations. The clergyperson must shift from the role of the competent expert to the role of the facilitator who helps the parishioner get to the expert. Making this shift gracefully requires that the clergyperson have considerable openness, a clear perception of his or her own abilities, and a secure sense of self-esteem.

These shifts may be difficult for both the clergyperson and the parishioner, and as a result there is often resistance to a referral, on one or both of their parts. This resistance, if not detected and dealt with promptly, can totally undermine the referral. This is what occurred in the following example—and in an unfortunately high percentage of referrals. (All case examples in this book, unless otherwise noted, are taken from the author's clinical files. Identifying data have been changed to maintain confidentiality.)

Dr. R, a psychiatrist, received a telephone call one day from Rabbi J, a resident of the same community, whom he had known for about two years. The rabbi had referred several congregants to Dr. R in the past, and their relationship was a friendly one. Rabbi J said that he had another person to refer to the doctor—this time, however, it was a personal friend, Mr. P. It appeared that Mr. P was quite depressed, and was also suffering from a significant medical illness which seemed to be related to his depression. Dr. R agreed that Mr. P was an appropriate person for referral.

Several days later, Mr. P telephoned the psychiatrist. He began the conversation, even before stating anything about his problem, by saying that he really didn't know what Dr. R could do for him. He then went on to ask a number of questions about the type of treatment Dr. R did. The doctor answered the questions and tried to be supportive, but he got the definite impression that Mr. P was very nervous, and had mixed feelings about making an appointment. Mr. P then asked Dr. R if he was a psychiatrist, and when the answer was given in the affirmative, he seemed quite surprised. This was quite striking to Dr. R because he was sure from his past experience that Rabbi J had given this information to Mr. P; the latter's failure to hear it was another indication of his anxiety. Mr. P then made the most significant statement of the conversation. He said, "Well, I called Rabbi J and he didn't have time to talk to me, so he gave me your name." Dr. R knew from his original discussion with Rabbi J that the rabbi had, in fact, spent a good deal of time with Mr. P, yet the statement suggested that Mr. P felt rejected and let down by his friend, and was rather angry as well.

At the end of the conversation, an appointment was set up. When the appointment time arrived, Mr. P failed to appear, and did not contact the doctor again.

The next section of this chapter will deal with ways of uncovering, understanding, and handling resistance to the referral.

Resistance to the Referral Process

The clergyperson making a referral should repeatedly think of the

following four questions:
1. Is the parishioner showing resistance?
2. If so, why is the resistance present?
3. Am I showing resistance?
4. If so, what is the reason?
We will consider each of these questions separately.

Question 1: Is the parishioner resisting?

Resistance can take many forms, from the most obvious to the extremely subtle. The parishioner may make a flat, direct refusal ("Sorry, Pastor, I just won't waste any money on a headshrinker") or a generalized statement of dislike ("Don't you know those psychologists are a bunch of phonies?"). These gross resistances are difficult to miss, but more subtle forms can sometimes go unnoticed.

The parishioner may agree superficially but may indicate through nonverbal behavior that he or she does not really agree at all. The parishioner may, for example, say "yes" but with a shake of the head indicating "no." The tone of voice which is used and the facial expressions which are displayed are important clues to underlying resistance. Sometimes the parishioner's overall behavior will be revealing: he may, for example, agree to the referral, write down the information on a piece of paper, and then walk out leaving the piece of paper behind.

Sometimes the parishioner may simply block out what has been said; he or she will not refuse the referral but will change the subject and act as if the suggestion was never made.

Another form of resistance is seen when the parishioner agrees with the suggestion but then immediately gives a reason why it cannot be acted on. ("That's great advice—I'd really like to talk to a psychiatrist, but. . . .") The "reason" is usually something else which stands in the way, often considerations of time or money.

A particularly powerful form of resistance is that in which the parishioner insists that he or she has complete faith in the clergyperson's abilities. ("But, Rabbi, I know you can handle this; after all, isn't this what you're trained to do?") The second part of the statement, which may be stated directly or implied, has the frequent effect of making the clergyperson feel vaguely guilty for "letting down" the parishioner. It is crucial that the clergyperson recognize such a maneuver as a manifestation of resistance, rather than a statement of fact. The clergyperson must be prepared to state, if necessary, that he or she is *not* trained to handle this problem, but would like to help the parishioner get to someone who is.

Sometimes resistance takes the form of an emotional outburst, the most common type being either dramatic anger or profuse crying. Such displays can stir up powerful feelings in the clergyperson: fear and counter-anger at the angry person, sympathy and guilt with the weeping parishioner. Here again, it is important that the clergyperson recognize these emotional outbursts as resistance and handle them as such, rather than simply responding from his or her own emotions. The most effective response to this situation is a calm, sympathetic statement which recognizes that the parishioner must be quite upset at the suggestion of a referral and invites him or her to talk more about the underlying feelings.

In some cases, as in the example of Mr. P, the parishioner may seem to accept the referral, but then fail to make an appointment, or fail to keep the appointment after it is made. If this occurs, the clergyperson should not abandon the effort. This development should be taken as an indication that resistance is present and that more discussion with the parishioner is necessary.

Question 2: Why is the parishioner resisting?

When the clergyperson sees resistance on the part of the parishioner, it is essential that the reasons for it be explored. It should be stated at the outset that in the vast majority of cases, individuals do not resist because of any conscious desire to create difficulties for the clergyperson. This may seem obvious to the reader, but it is important to remember it, for in the heat of an emotional scene with a resisting parishioner, one can sometimes lose sight of this fact and unwittingly react in anger. Such a reaction is a sure way to doom a referral and damage a helping relationship.

One of the most common reasons for resistance is fear. The parishioner may be afraid of the professional to whom he or she is being referred; there may be fear of forced medications or hospitalization. Most people today have heard disturbing stories about psychiatrists, mental hospitals, and psychotherapists in general, and these stories may be the basis for the fear. A member of the parishioner's family or a friend may have had a negative experience with a mental health professional. In addition, the individual may be afraid of any social stigma which may result from treatment.

In these situations, the clergyperson's own attitudes are extremely important. If he or she believes that there is no stigma involved, and that the professional to whom the referral is made is competent and has personal integrity, the parishioner's fears should not be difficult to deal with. It is most important to ask directly about these fears, to listen to them carefully, and to acknowledge the parishioner's discomfort. Misconceptions should be clarified and reassurance should be given, but only after the individual has had an adequate chance to ventilate feelings. Reassurance which is given too hastily can sometimes convey the opposite message and increase the parishioner's fears that there really *is* something of which to be afraid.

Sometimes the resistance does not stem from any fears or misconceptions but rather reflects the parishioner's feeling of being rejected by, or disappointed in, the clergyperson. In these cases, the individual has come with the expectation—usually quite unrealistic—that the clergyperson can provide solutions to all problems. When the clergyperson indicates that this is not so, the parishioner is likely to feel rejected and angry and to express this anger through resistance to the referral. This situation is more difficult for the clergyperson to deal with, because it involves confronting a negative feeling, but this confrontation is essential if the referral is to succeed. The parishioner must be asked directly, but supportively and empathetically, whether he or she is feeling disappointed or angry. The clergyperson must be prepared, if necessary, to sit through some emotional language and some unfair criticisms in response to the question, without reacting angrily or defensively.

"Sitting through" an angry outburst with a disappointed parishioner can be a painful experience. It may be of some comfort to the clergyperson to know that physicians often have the same uncomfortable experience when making referrals. When magical expectations are not met, a flood of feelings is invariably released. But while these moments are painful, they also carry within them the potential for growth and maturation of the parishioner. If the clergyperson can remain calm, supportive, and realistic during this experience, the parishioner may be able to abandon some of his or her distorted expectations and accept a realistic, human relationship, even with its inevitable limitations. In other words, the clergyperson can show the parishioner that reality is ultimately more worthwhile than fantasy. On yet another level, a person who has trouble recognizing another's limitations often has great fears of facing his or her own. If the clergyperson can demonstrate a calm, realistic acceptance of his or her own limits even when "under fire," the parishioner may be able to begin doing likewise.

If these negative feelings are not confronted and aired, the parishioner is likely not to follow through on the referral, as in the case of Mr. P. Even if the individual does follow through and begin therapy elsewhere, the negative feelings are likely to be carried over into the therapy. If this occurs, it will be difficult for the treatment to be successful.

Another very subtle, but very important, source of resistance lies in the parishioner's sensing the clergyperson's own resistance and responding to it in kind. This phenomenon will be discussed in greater detail when we consider the clergyperson's resistance in the next section of this chapter.

Finally, it is obviously true that in some cases, the resistance may be due to very real practical factors—insufficient funds, lack of transportation, inability to arrange child care, etc. In a few cases these problems may really be insoluble, but most of the time a resourceful clergyperson can find a way around them. However, the most important point is to resist the temptation to become angry or impatient in the process.

This is not meant to be an exhaustive list of the sources of resistance; many others probably exist. The essential step for the clergyperson is to ask the question "why?" and take the question seriously. Once this is done, even the most complex causes of resistance can be unraveled and dealt with.

Question 3: Is the clergyperson resisting?

In addition to being aware of the parishioner's resistance, the clergyperson must be aware of his or her own as well. The manifestations of the clergyperson's resistance can be as subtle as the parishioner's, and its recognition calls for a high degree of self-awareness. This recognition is extremely important, for if the clergyperson is showing ambivalence or negative feelings about the referral, it is almost certain that the parishioner will sense those feelings.

The clergyperson, like the parishioner, can give nonverbal negative messages which contradict and overshadow the content of what is said. Tone of voice, body posture, or facial expression can communicate the message that the clergyperson is uncomfortable or reluctant about the referral. Resistance can show itself in other forms of behavior as well; in one case, for example, a pastor realized after a parishioner had left his office that he had given the parishioner the incorrect address for the local Mental Health Center. This was not a matter of insufficient knowledge—the pastor knew quite well where the center was located—but his resistance had intervened.

The clergyperson's resistance can also surface in the form of implications to the parishioner that the treatment will fail or that the individual will not like the agency or practitioner to whom he or she is being referred. Consider the following statement, made by a pastor to a parishioner:

> "I think you should see Dr. X. He's a good man and he will try to help you—but remember, if he can't help you, or if you don't like the treatment, make sure you call me back."

The clergyperson's desire to be helpful is quite evident, but is there not a definite implication behind the last part of the statement? The pastor is almost saying that he *expects* the parishioner not to like the doctor and expects that he will return to the pastor. In other words, the unspoken message—which may be totally out of the pastor's awareness—is, "Don't go; stay with me." When such a message is given, the chances are quite high that the individual will, in fact, call the clergyperson after the first visit to the doctor and say that he is dissatisfied. The clergyperson is then left with a failure of referral and with a parishioner whose problems have not been helped. Most unfortunate of all, the clergyperson may have no idea why the referral failed to help the person.

Question 4: Why is the clergyperson resisting?

The next step in this process involves some self-examination on the part of the clergyperson to find the source of his or her resistance. One of the major causes of resistance has already been touched on: Making a referral often calls upon the clergyperson to admit that he or she is not able to fulfill the expectations of the parishioner. For some clergy this is relatively easy to do, while for others it is quite difficult.

In some cases, the problem may lie with the clergyperson's *own* self-expectations—not the parishioner's expectations—and the inability to admit limitations. What is ultimately involved here is the clergyperson's self-image and the degree to which his or her self-esteem is dependent on the parishioner's opinions.

These issues are certainly not unique to the clergy; they also apply to every mental health professional in his or her relationship with patients or clients. Indeed, they apply to all human relationships, but most people do not have their self-image and self-esteem tested as frequently, or as painfully, as do those in the helping professions.

Another source of resistance in the clergyperson has to do with political and social considerations within the congregation. The clergyperson may feel pressured to continue seeing the parishioner rather than to make a referral. The troubled person may be an influential member of the congregation, or the relative of an influential member, and the clergyperson may fear that a referral will arouse feelings that will eventually result in political problems or social discomfort.

If such fears are lurking in the background, the clergyperson will do well to bring them into full awareness and think them through carefully. Like any effective leader, the clergyperson must be careful to maintain good relations with as many constituents as possible. With tact and discretion, many of these politically delicate situations can be resolved to everyone's satisfaction. But in those few instances where a choice must be made, the welfare of the individual should take precedence over political considerations.

A third possible source of the clergyperson's resistance may be problems in the relationship with the practitioner or institution to which the parishioner is being referred. The clergyperson's feelings about the practitioner or agency are extremely important in determining whether or not the parishioner will follow through. If there is any feeling of dissatisfaction on the clergyperson's part, if there is any doubt in his or her mind about the competence or integrity of the person or agency, the referral should not be made until those feelings have been resolved. If the referral is attempted while those feelings are still active, the clergyperson's ambivalence is likely to be communicated to the parishioner and the referral may be undermined.

There may be many other sources of the clergyperson's resistance in addition to those discussed above. Here again, the essential thing is to ask "Why?" and to pursue the answer, even when that process is an uncomfortable one.

To summarize: Resistance is a very important factor in the referral process, both on the part of the clergyperson and the parishioner. The ability to recognize, understand, and talk about resistance is one of the clergyperson's main keys to success in making a referral.

Consultation

In this chapter, we have been considering the situation in which a person is referred to a professional for ongoing treatment or counseling. There is another option, however, which is open to the clergyperson: a psychiatrist or other mental health professional can be used as a one-time consultant, without a full referral being made. A consultant can be very helpful in cases where the clergyperson has difficulty determining whether or not a referral is necessary, or in instances where there is a great deal of resistance which has resulted in a stalemate. A consultant can also be useful when problems or roadblocks arise in the ongoing counseling which the clergyperson is doing.

A consultant should be chosen primarily on the basis of training and experience with the problem which the clergyperson is facing. The same consultant will not necessarily be able to help in all situations. Expertise should be the primary criterion, but it is also very important that the consultant be someone whom the clergyperson trusts and with whom he or she can speak openly about feelings and hesitations. For this reason, many clergy have found that it is easier to use a consultant who is completely outside of the congregational structure.

Choosing a consultant should be done in the same manner as choosing a practitioner to whom to refer. The clergyperson should ideally have meetings with several private practitioners in the community and ask each of them whatever questions are pertinent. The clergyperson should ask in each case if the professional would be willing to act as a consultant; not all practitioners are interested in this type of service. The discussion should also include questions of fees and the mechanics of setting up a consultation.

Like referral, consultation is a process which requires time, thought, and skill, and a consultation will be most effective if it is set up carefully in advance. The process begins when the clergyperson becomes aware of a problem or question in the course of dealing with an emotionally troubled parishioner. Before taking any further action, the clergyperson should try to clarify the problem or question in his or her own mind as much as possible. At this point a consultant should be selected.

The next step in the consultation process should be a conversation between the clergyperson and the consultant. The latter should be told the nature of the problem and the questions which need to be answered. In some cases, the consultant may be able to answer the questions and give sufficient help during the conversation, and the process will be completed at this point. In other cases, however, the consultant will want to meet directly with the parishioner for one or two visits. The clergyperson must then do the most delicate and important part of the consultation process: the presentation of the idea to the parishioner.

A consultation is similar to a referral in that the same resistances can be encountered in each situation. It is essential that the clergyperson examine his or her own resistances, if there are any, and put them to rest before broaching the subject to the parishioner. It may be helpful for the clergyperson to remember that consultation is a very common and long-standing practice in medical settings; in fact, medical ethics *require* that one seek consultation when unsure of what is the best course to follow with a patient.

When raising the subject with the parishioner, the clergyperson can take the lead by stating openly that he or she wants to help but is having some difficulty seeing the best way to do so. The consultant should be presented as an adviser who will help the clergyperson to be more effective. Basic information about the consultant and his or her professional background should then be given. It is usually best to make the initial statement relatively brief and then allow time for the parishioner's questions and emotional responses. The resistances which arise at this point should be recognized, understood, and discussed in exactly the same manner as the resistances to referral. The clergyperson should maintain an attitude of support and understanding, should stand firm in the recommendation, but should also be prepared to allow ample time for discussion and for the parishioner to make up his or her mind.

If resistances are handled adequately and the parishioner agrees to the consultation, the next step in the process is the setting up of an appointment with the consultant. It is always more desirable that the parishioner contact the consultant directly to make these arrangements, rather than the clergyperson doing it. From a practical point of view, the parishioner is in the best position to set up a suitable time and obtain directions to the consultant's office. It is also helpful for the parishioner to make this brief contact, so that when he or she goes to the office, the consultant will not be approached as a total stranger. From yet another point of view, the parishioner's willingness to make this contact is a measure of his or her motivation; conversely, the individual's failure to take this step is a sign of resistance and indicates that more discussion with the clergyperson is necessary.

After the parishioner's appointment with the consultant, the usual procedure is that the consultant contacts the clergyperson for further discussion. A direct conversation, by telephone or in person, is always more fruitful than a written report. In the discussion, the consultant should answer the clergyperson's original questions. According to the situation, the consultant may also recommend changes in the clergyperson's general approach, specific techniques of counseling, or referral to a mental health professional.

The final step in the consultation process involves the clergyperson discussing the consultation experience with the parishioner and implementing the consultant's suggestions. The discussion of the experience with the parishioner is very important for several reasons. On the simplest level, it demonstrates the clergyperson's concern about what may have been an anxiety-provoking experience. Furthermore, the parishioner may have some distorted perceptions of what the consultant said, and the clergyperson is in a position to modify these perceptions, thereby making it easier for the individual to accept the consultant's advice. Finally, the discussion gives the parishioner the message that the consultation was not an isolated event but is an integral and integrated part of the clergyperson's overall plan of counseling.

References for Further Reading

Lee, R. R., "Referral as an Act of Pastoral Care," *Journal of Pastoral Care*, vol. 30 (1976), pp. 186-197.

Clinebell, Howard J., Jr., *Basic Types of Pastoral Counseling*. New York: Abingdon Press, 1966.

Klink, T., "The Referral: Helping People Focus Their Needs," *Pastoral Psychology*, vol. 13 (1962), pp. 10-15.

Kimsey, Larry R., and Roberts, Jean L. *Referring the Psychiatric Patient*. Springfield, Ill.: Charles C. Thomas, Publisher, 1973. (This book, though written for physicians, has useful sections for the clergy, particularly chapters 3, 4, and 5.)

 THREE

Dealing with the Psychotic Person

The clergyperson who is involved with the day-to-day leadership of a congregation is likely to encounter some individuals who are strikingly strange in their behavior and thinking. Some of these people will prove to be simply eccentric personalities, but others may be suffering from a treatable psychiatric condition known as "psychosis." The number of psychotic individuals whom the clergyperson encounters will probably be quite small, but even one of these very troubled people can cause a great deal of discomfort and distress to the clergyperson, and sometimes to the entire congregation. In addition, these individuals are often quite difficult to refer for professional help, even though the need for such help seems obvious. An understanding of psychosis and how to deal with it will help the clergyperson to minimize the discomfort and will increase the chances of getting help for the psychotic person.

The Definition of Psychosis

A psychotic person is one who is out of touch with reality to a major degree. The qualifying phrase "to a major degree" is important because of the fact that every person, at one time or another, exhibits some unrealistic thinking or behavior. In the nonpsychotic person, however, these traits are usually quite limited and do not dominate the individual's life. The nonpsychotic person is also able to recognize unrealistic thoughts and behavior when they are pointed out and, with some help, is often able to change them. The psychotic person, on the other hand, does not realize that he or she is out of touch with reality, and this makes such an individual difficult to help. The psychotic person is dominated by unrealistic ideas and behavior and is crippled by them to such an extent that day-to-day functioning is severely impaired.

It is usually not very difficult to recognize a psychotic person, and one need not always be a mental health professional to make this assessment. Most psychotic people are brought for help by lay people around them—by family or friends—who intuitively recognize that they are quite ill. The psychotic person's lack of contact with reality is evident in his or her *behavior, emotional display,* and *thinking,* and the determination of psychosis is based on an evaluation of these three spheres of functioning. Each of these will be discussed in some detail.

Behavior

The behavior of a psychotic person may at times be grossly bizarre or strikingly strange. The psychotic man may walk around in a heavy winter coat in the middle of summer, and the psychotic woman may wear her hair and makeup in a way which is obviously bizarre. Some psychotic individuals assume strange postures or make unusual gestures and facial grimaces. They may also do dangerous things without realizing that they are in danger, such as walking in the middle of a busy intersection without watching the cars going by.

More often, however, the psychotic person does not behave in a grossly bizarre way, but rather in a socially inappropriate manner. Psychotic people are not able to follow the rules of social interaction that others take for granted—those rules which are so important in keeping everyday relationships going smoothly. A psychotic person may talk too loudly, too long, or about subjects which most people would consider inappropriate for the situation. Psychotic individuals may make telephone calls very late at night, or knock on the doors of total strangers. Very often, the psychotic individual first comes to the attention of a clergyperson through some type of socially inappropriate behavior.

It must always be kept in mind that the psychotic person does not recognize the inappropriate nature of his or her acts. If this fact is forgotten, the clergyperson may become upset and angry at a psychotic individual who seems to be simply refusing to follow the rules of common social interaction.

Emotional Display

Psychotic individuals have an unusual way of expressing emotion. They may, first of all, exhibit what is referred to as "flattened affect": the person may talk about an idea which others would expect to be emotionally loaded; yet the individual's face may show no expression whatever. The emotion is "flat," and the observer cannot tell what the speaker is feeling.

Another characteristic of the emotional display of psychotic people is that it may be inappropriate to the subject matter. There is often a lack of agreement between the content of what the psychotic person is saying and the emotion which he or she is showing. The person may, for example, laugh while describing something which to the observer sounds quite fearful or sad.

Every nonpsychotic person, particularly at times of emotional stress, may have moments of emotional flatness or inappropriateness. In the psychotic individual, however, this is an almost constant state of affairs. Here again, he or she may have no awareness of the nature of this emotional display and is not making any deliberate attempt to mislead others.

Thinking

Psychotic people do not follow the usual logical thinking patterns to which we are accustomed. The thoughts which they express often do not follow a logical sequence and are difficult for the observer to understand. Psychotic people may also develop ideas which are not logical, yet are fixed and not amenable to modification through rational discussion. These ideas are referred to by psychiatrists as "delusions."

There are two general types of delusions which one finds among psychotic people. The first is the *persecutory* delusion, in which the individual believes that he or she is being controlled or influenced by some outside force which is bent on doing harm. The outside force may be an individual, an organization, a machine, or a supernatural being.

The psychotic person often portrays himself or herself as a helpless victim, and frequently a very angry one.

Second is the *grandiose* delusion, in which the psychotic person believes that he or she is very special or very famous, possessing extraordinary talents. The fact that others do not see these special talents makes no impression on the psychotic person, other than to "prove" that others are either stupid and prejudiced, or are part of a conspiracy to conceal the truth.

There is one type of grandiose delusion that is particularly important to mention here: the idea that God is in direct touch with the individual. There are a number of psychotic people who voice such ideas about God, and these people are likely to approach a clergyperson. It is obviously very important that the clergyperson be able to distinguish between the individual who has had a true religious experience and the psychotic person who is having a religious delusion. In most cases, the distinction is not very difficult to make. If one looks carefully at the overall picture of the individual's behavior, emotional display, and quality of thinking, one can usually make a distinction between psychosis and health. In those cases where the distinction is difficult to make, a psychiatric consultation can be very helpful.

Hallucinations

Another feature of the psychotic state is the presence of hallucinations. The technical definition of a hallucination is "a sensory experience in the absence of any real stimulus to produce that experience." The most common hallucinations are *auditory*—the individual hears sounds or voices when there is no one present who could be producing those sounds or voices. Hallucinations may also be *visual, tactile* (feeling sensations on the skin), or *olfactory* (smelling something, usually something unpleasant). At the onset of a psychosis, the individual is usually frightened by the hallucinations; as time goes on, however, he or she may grow accustomed to them, and may even enjoy them.

The clergyperson may be approached by a hallucinating individual who believes that he or she is hearing the voice of God, or seeing divinely inspired visions. Here again, it is crucial to distinguish between that which is truly religious and that which is psychotic. An overall evaluation usually will point to the correct answer, and consultation should be obtained when there is any doubt.

Identifying the Psychotic

The following example will demonstrate a number of the features of psychosis which have been discussed above. In this instance, the psychosis was long-standing and was quite difficult to deal with. One should not infer from this that all psychoses are this severe; the case was chosen deliberately to illustrate the more extreme problems of dealing with psychotic people.

Mr. A, an intelligent young man from a middle-class family, became mentally ill while in his late twenties. At that time he was employed by a large corporation in a position with a promising future. Because of his illness, however, he became unable to do his work, and his relationship with his superiors and co-workers deteriorated. He was finally terminated from his job and shortly thereafter was admitted to a psychiatric hospital. He remained there for a short time and was then discharged to be treated as an outpatient. After several months he discontinued his outpatient treatment. The members of his immediate family had all either died or moved out of the community, and he had no close friends to turn to for help. He went onto public assistance and lived alone in a rented room in a run-down part of the city.

Over the next year, Mr. A developed the idea that a number of people throughout the world had conspired to cause him to lose his employment. This group of people included a number of internationally known figures in his field, who in reality had never even met him. In addition, Mr. A came to believe that it was his mission to be in touch with the heads of state of various countries, and to advise them about important political decisions. He actually sent long telegrams to different heads of government, giving advice on world problems.

About two years after his hospitalization, Mr. A returned to the church in which he had grown up. Although his family was no longer there, many members of the congregation remembered him, and at first they welcomed him back. He attended services occasionally but would always sit alone. His facial expression for the most part was blank. After the initial welcome, the members of the congregation tended to keep away from him.

Soon Mr. A began making loud comments during the services.

The congregation politely ignored him, but people began feeling more and more uncomfortable. On one occasion he stood up during the sermon and made some angry, quite illogical statements about the pastor. He was asked politely to leave, but the following week he was back again.

Mr. A's behavior grew more disturbing and inappropriate as the weeks passed. One Sunday, for example, he arrived at the church in a taxi just as the service was ending. He walked up to the pastor, who was standing near the door, and demanded abruptly that the pastor pay his taxi fare, since he himself had no money. The angry cab driver confirmed that Mr. A had indeed run up a fare of $30. In order to avoid an unpleasant scene, several members of the congregation paid the bill, but the incident left everyone feeling frustrated and angry.

Face-to-face conversations with Mr. A were unnerving and generally futile. He always seemed to make statements which were unanswerable; and when a direct question was put to him, he always managed to evade answering it, either by giving an illogical reply or by making a hostile comment and walking away.

As time passed, feelings about Mr. A grew stronger and stronger among the congregation. A small minority wanted to bar him from the premises altogether, but these people were overruled by the majority who felt that his obvious illness ruled out such a move. According to the latter view, the church was a place of refuge for afflicted, lonely people, and Mr. A certainly fit that category. Everyone, however, agreed that something had to be done, yet exactly what was unclear. The congregation looked to the pastor for an answer.

We will return to the case of Mr. A later in this chapter.

The causes of psychosis will not be discussed in any great detail here and are not essential for the clergyperson to know. It will suffice to say that a large number of illnesses, both medical and psychiatric, can cause a person to become psychotic. An additional cause of psychosis is drug abuse, particularly the abuse of amphetamines ("speed," diet pills, "uppers") and the hallucinogenic drugs (LSD, PCP, mescaline, etc.). Schizophrenia, probably the most feared of the mental illnesses, is only one cause of psychosis. It is by no means true that every psychotic person is schizophrenic with all which that entails.

Some types of psychosis are long-standing, while other types are brief and transient. The great majority of psychoses, however, are treatable, and therefore one can approach a psychotic person with a sense of optimism. If effective interventions are made, most psychotic people can be significantly helped, and in some cases they can be completely cured.

In past generations, psychotic people were considered to be qualitatively different from the rest of the human race and were often treated accordingly. In the last hundred years, however, we have come to understand that psychosis is the response of certain individuals to overwhelming emotional stress. Underneath the bizarre exterior, the psychotic person is struggling with many of the same issues that all people face—issues such as self-esteem, dependency needs, aggression, and personal identity. What makes the psychotic person different is that he or she lacks the psychological apparatus for making meaningful constructive sense out of inner feelings. The distorted thinking and behavior of the psychotic person represents the individual's desperate attempts to make *some* sort of sense—however illogical it may be—out of these feelings and experiences.

How is the clergyperson likely to come in contact with a psychotic individual? It is unlikely that the psychotic person will come forward and ask directly for professional help, for, as we have seen, the person usually does not recognize the need for help. It is much more likely that he or she will be brought, often under duress, to the clergyperson by family or friends. In other cases, the clergyperson may be asked to visit the psychotic person. A third possibility is the most disturbing: the clergyperson may suddenly realize that he or she is involved in the psychotic individual's delusions. This is what occurred in the case of Mr. A.

One day, several weeks after Mr. A had returned to the congregation, the pastor received a letter from him in the mail. The letter was full of hostile, graphic language, and in it Mr. A accused the pastor of ruining his life. It was obvious from the letter that the pastor was one of the people who Mr. A believed had caused him to lose his job. In addition to this, there were other accusations, some of them quite bizarre. Mr. A wrote, for example, that several young women in the congregation, at the pastor's direction, had made "sexual advances" to him. He also stated that the pastor had been responsible for mistreatment that Mr. A had received at the time of his hospitalization.

What was most upsetting to the pastor was that the letter was so unexpected and so out of line with the pastor's perception of his relationship with Mr. A. His involvement with the A family had begun many years earlier when Mr. A's father had died unexpectedly. The pastor had spent much time with the family and had continued to counsel them over the years. Since Mr. A's illness, the pastor had gone out of his way to visit him in the hospital and to keep abreast of what was happening to him.

This letter was only the first of many letters and phone calls to the pastor from Mr. A over the next year. Mr. A seemed to have an endless list of grievances and demands. At one point he wrote in a letter that the pastor should pay him one million dollars to make up for all the injustices which were done to him. The very absurdity of these assertions made them impossible to answer.

A psychotic person who forms a delusion usually incorporates into it either people who are known from everyday life, or authority figures who have symbolic meaning. The clergyperson often fits both of these categories and is therefore a prime candidate for incorporation into a psychotic delusion. (Doctors are also prime candidates, for the same reasons.) When this happens, the delusion may exist "underground" at first, developing slowly over a long period of time until it is finally revealed.

Dealing with the Psychotic Person

With these general considerations in mind, we can now turn to a discussion of some specific guidelines for clergy to follow when dealing with a psychotic person. After presenting these guidelines, we will return for a final discussion of the case of Mr. A.

Guideline 1 : Recognize the illness.

The first step in the helping process is the recognition that the psychotic person is ill. This step seems obvious but is often not so easy in practice. In order to recognize the illness, the clergyperson must overcome his or her own resistance to this idea and frequently must work against the resistance of the psychotic person's family and friends. It is not unusual for the latter to continue in their denial of the illness, even when the evidence seems overwhelming. This is particularly true when the psychotic person is a highly respected or influential member of the congregation.

In these situations, the clergyperson may be the only one who is in a position to point out firmly, but sympathetically, that the individual is ill and needs professional help. As was noted above, this can be said with an air of optimism, since the majority of psychotic people can be helped by psychiatric treatment. And while the label of "mental illness" is frightening to many people, it carries a potential benefit for the one who is psychotic: others are more likely to be sympathetic and helpful if they view the psychotic person as "ill," rather than as an irritating "troublemaker."

Guideline 2: Clarify the goal.

The clergyperson who deals with a psychotic individual must always keep the goal of the intervention clearly defined. Unless the clergyperson has had special training, the goal is not to treat or counsel the psychotic person, but rather to get him or her to the place where treatment can occur—in other words, to make a referral.

This implies, first of all, that the clergyperson must have certain information readily available. The name, address, and telephone number of the nearest mental health center, general hospital, or psychiatrist are indispensable. If a psychiatrist in private practice is to be contacted, the clergyperson should know in advance whether or not the psychiatrist is available for emergencies during nights and weekends.

The clergyperson may feel some pressure from family or associates of the psychotic individual who do not want a referral to be made. These people are usually motivated by embarrassment or fear, and they often have the fantasy that the clergyperson can somehow "cure" the psychotic individual. If such a situation arises, the clergyperson must withstand the pressure and make a clear statement that he or she will do all that is necessary to help the psychotic person obtain treatment but that the treatment will ultimately have to be done by others. At the same time, the clergyperson should be open to hearing the family's or friends' concerns and fears about psychiatric treatment. The clergyperson should have enough acquaintance with mental health care to be able to dispel the fears which are unfounded and acknowledge those concerns which are realistic. The time spent in discussion with the family and associates of the psychotic person is extremely important in determining whether or not the individual will eventually receive appropriate help.

One of the greatest mistakes that a clergyperson can make is to be drawn into counseling or "treating" a psychotic person without having had special training. This often leads to worsening of the psychosis and sometimes results in outright physical harm. What is being said here is that the clergyperson must know his or her limitations, must be prepared to declare them, and must resist the temptation to exceed them, even under pressure. This same principle applies to all mental health professionals. We must stay within our limitations not only for our own protection but also as a fundamental part of our ethical obligation to those who seek our help. When a clergyperson exceeds the boundaries of competence, it is ultimately the psychotic person who suffers the most.

The clergyperson then has the difficult task of convincing the psychotic individual to accept a referral. This may take a long period of time—weeks or even months—and a good deal of energy may have to be devoted to this task. This consideration leads to a third guideline.

Guideline 3: Obtain consultation.

The clergyperson should never attempt to deal with a psychotic individual alone but should always call for advice and consultation from a psychiatrist or mental health center in the community. Psychotic people have a mysterious quality about them that is frightening, yet very magnetic at the same time, and it is easy to become drawn into and isolated in a relationship with such a person. When this occurs, the clergyperson may begin to lose his or her own sense of reality and may start to take dangerous risks which can lead to tragedy.

It is also easy for the clergyperson to fall into the trap of feeling that he or she is expected to carry the burden of a psychotic person alone, as part of the religious calling, and may experience guilt at needing to ask for help. The congregation's unrealistic expectations may feed this feeling and increase the guilt even further. If these feelings begin to occur, the clergyperson should seek consultation and support right away, either from a mental health professional or from a trusted and experienced clergy colleague. Having frequent discussion and consultation is the best way to guard against misfortune and maximize the chances of recovery for the psychotic person.

An example will illustrate these points.

Mr. O approached his priest, Father M, one Sunday after the service and asked if they could have a few minutes together. Fr. M agreed, and Mr. O proceeded to talk about his belief that his house was being "haunted" by "spirits of the Devil." He described hearing "the voice of the Devil" talking to him and giving him instructions. He also felt that he was being controlled by the Devil, who was "making" him do certain things. He asked if Fr. M could perform an exorcism to rid the house of the Satanic spirits.

Fr. M noted that Mr. O was disheveled in appearance and that his facial expressions were unusual, but there was something fascinating about him. The priest spent some time talking with Mr. O and finally asked him to return the following day. Part of Fr. M's motivation in doing this was that he himself was interested in the occult.

On the following day, Mr. O returned. Fr. M again was vaguely aware that Mr. O behaved strangely and that his thoughts did not really make sense. Nonetheless, he was again fascinated by the story and agreed to the request for an exorcism.

The ceremony was performed several days later, and Mr. O reported to Fr. M that the "voices of the Devil" had ceased. The priest was relieved and hoped that the incident was over; he was becoming more and more uncomfortable about Mr. O. One week later, however, Mr. O called again. He sounded even more disorganized in his thinking than before. He stated that the voices had returned; this time, however, they were telling him to kill his children because they were "sinners." He added that he now believed that the voice was that of God, and that he had to obey the command.

At this point, Fr. M finally sought consultation from a local mental health center. Mr. O was committed to a hospital and a tragedy was averted.

The clergyperson's primary objective in working with a psychotic individual should be to gain that person's trust and confidence. This is difficult to accomplish, but the next two guidelines will offer some basic principles to be followed in working toward this goal.

Guideline 4: Do not debate delusions.

One should never try to argue a psychotic person out of delusions, no matter how well-intentioned the attempt may be. There are two reasons for avoiding this type of debate. The first is that it simply will not work. Delusional ideas are supported by an idiosyncratic system of logic in which the psychotic person can find an argument to answer any assertion which is made. Debating with a psychotic person over a delusion is like trying to fight a cloud of dust with a shotgun.

A psychotic young man came to the Emergency Room of a hospital and told the nurse on duty that he was dead. He was seen by a number of nurses and doctors, and to each of them he repeated with absolute certainty that he was dead. One physician finally hit on an ingenious way of proving his point. He asked the young man if he thought that dead men bleed, and the young man replied that they do not. The doctor then took out a pin and pricked the young man's finger, and it began to bleed. The young man stared at his finger in amazement for a moment and then exclaimed, "Well, I'll be damned—dead men *do* bleed!"

The second reason for avoiding debate over delusions is that such debate will cause distrust on the part of the psychotic person, who will not perceive the clergyperson's good intentions. To the psychotic individual, it will only appear that he or she is being opposed and not taken seriously. The clergyperson who persists in such debate will succeed only in being incorporated into the delusion, thereby strengthening it even further.

Guideline 5: Maintain honesty.

The clergyperson should never try to humor a psychotic individual or pretend to understand when he or she really does not. Psychotic persons have an uncanny ability to sense when they are being humored or fooled, and they will see right through the attempt. The clergyperson who tries to use deception will destroy the psychotic person's trust and damage the relationship.

It is important to remember that the psychotic individual is constantly watching very closely to see if other people are dealing honestly. Many of these people grew up in families where they were constantly being given confusing messages and contradictory communications. It is very difficult for most psychotics to trust anyone, and the clergyperson will have to win the psychotic person's trust by demonstrating honesty over and over again.

Those who come in contact with a psychotic person are often very hesitant to admit to the individual that they do not understand what he or she is trying to say, or that they do not know the answer to the individual's questions. The common fear is that such an admission will make the psychotic person more confused or more angry. In fact, however, this frank admission can have a very positive effect, because it demonstrates that the speaker is willing to swallow pride and be honest. The statement should be made in a calm, nonthreatening manner, without anger or defensiveness, simply stated as a matter of fact. The clergyperson should remember that a moment of truth is extremely valuable to the psychotic person, regardless of the content of that truth. Such a moment can be an important foundation stone in building a therapeutic relationship.

One of the implications of this ground rule of honesty is that one should never conceal from a psychotic person plans or decisions which will have a direct bearing on the individual. This can become a difficult issue for the clergyperson. Family or friends of the psychotic individual may make plans with the clergyperson and may want these plans to be kept secret. They may want the clergyperson to pay a pastoral visit to the individual, but to conceal the fact that the visit is being made at the family's request. The clergyperson will have to use judgment in each individual case, but as a general rule, this type of deception should be avoided. The keeping of secrets will undermine the basic trust which is such an important part of the pastoral relationship with the psychotic person.

The key to making a successful referral is to maintain a mixture of honesty and empathy and at the same time to keep the goal clearly in mind. The clergyperson must keep repeating—calmly, yet firmly—that the psychotic person could benefit from professional help, and that the clergyperson will do everything possible to assist in getting that help.

Guideline 6: Set limits.

It is absolutely essential when working with a psychotic individual that the clergyperson not allow himself or herself to be hurt or taken advantage of unfairly. As has been pointed out, the psychotic person is not able to follow the usual rules of social interaction and may try in many ways to take advantage of the clergyperson, to make excessive demands of time, or to invade privacy. In some cases, the psychotic person may be very hostile, or even physically threatening. It is crucial that the clergyperson carry on a process of continual self-monitoring. At the point where he or she begins to feel threatened or taken advantage of, active measures should be taken to limit or stop the psychotic person's actions.

This setting of limits is necessary not only for the clergyperson's protection, but for the sake of the psychotic individual as well. If the clergyperson allows himself or herself to be injured or abused, he or she may respond with irritation or rejection, and this will ultimately hurt the psychotic person. In addition, the psychotic individual who is allowed to inflict harm is likely to be overcome with guilt over the act and may break off the relationship altogether. If the guilt is severe enough, the individual may even become suicidal.

The clergyperson should follow some simple but valuable rules when dealing with a psychotic person who is frightening or hostile. Meetings with such a person should not be held in an empty building or late at night; the clergyperson should make sure that there are other people nearby and, if necessary, should keep the office door open during the meeting or have a third person in the room. If the psychotic person asks why this is being done, the clergyperson should state simply and calmly that he or she is concerned for safety and does not want anything harmful to happen to anyone. Here again, honesty is the most important consideration, and the clergyperson's realistic concern can be most reassuring to the psychotic individual.

Unfair intrusions into the clergyperson's time and private life should also be limited. The best way for the clergyperson to explain why this behavior must be stopped is to state that the intrusion makes him or her very uncomfortable and therefore not able to be of help. This should be said in a nondefensive manner, with both concern and firmness. The clergyperson should also offer an alternative course of action which accomplishes the psychotic person's goal in a more acceptable manner. For example, if a psychotic individual continually telephones the clergyperson's home late at night, the clergyperson's strategy should be first to explain that these calls are disturbing and therefore prevent him or her from being helpful. An alternative should then be offered: the person should be told that calls can be made to the office, during regular hours, or that an appointment can be made for a visit.

Once the reason has been explained and an alternative has been offered, the clergyperson should set the limit firmly and maintain it consistently. In the example of the late-night caller, the limit setting might involve the clergyperson refusing to accept calls after a certain hour and even taking the phone off the hook for several nights if the calls continue. This may seem unfair at first glance, but the more important consideration is that the clergyperson has an obligation to help the psychotic individual maintain some realistic self-control. Consistency is absolutely essential here; any ambiguity or inconsistency will be very confusing to the psychotic person and may lead to worsening of the symptoms.

The psychotic individual may become angry when limits are set, but the clergyperson should not be deterred by this anger. If the clergyperson stands by the limits, offers fair alternatives, and maintains a calm, concerned approach, a trusting relationship with the psychotic individual can eventually be established.

Involuntary Hospitalization

Up to this point, we have been considering ways to motivate a psychotic individual to seek help voluntarily. This is the most desirable course, since treatment is always more effective when a person agrees voluntarily to participate. But in certain cases, when the psychotic person is clearly dangerous either to self or to others, it may be necessary to institute a hospitalization against the person's will.

Involuntary commitment to a hospital is a legal process, and every state has its own laws and procedures for carrying it out. It is well worth the clergyperson's while to find out what the procedures are in his or her own state. The best place to turn for this information is to the nearest Community Mental Health Center or to any psychiatrist. The specifics will vary from state to state, but the general rule usually is that a psychotic person can be committed to a hospital if he or she has shown clear evidence of being dangerous to self or others. In many states the procedure involves testimony from a concerned lay person who has observed firsthand the dangerous behavior of the psychotic individual.

It is important that the clergyperson have some understanding of these matters, for two reasons. First, this information can be valuable in advising the family and friends of a psychotic person about involuntary commitment, should this become necessary. A second reason is that the clergyperson may personally witness the psychotic person's violent or suicidal behavior and may therefore be in a position to testify in a commitment hearing.

The decision of whether or not to come forth and testify in such a proceeding can be a difficult one. Many people are afraid to testify, out of fear that the person being committed will be angry and seek revenge. There have been cases where committed people felt very angry at those who had testified and a few cases in which an act of revenge occurred. But one must always weigh the possible benefits against the risks. The great majority of people who are committed against their will are ultimately helped by their treatment and do not bear a grudge against those who testified in the commitment hearing. The clergyperson may be in the position of being the only one who can testify, the only one who has actually seen violent or suicidal behavior. This requires courage, but it may be the only way that the psychotic person can be helped.

The issues discussed here should help us to understand what happened in the case of Mr. A.

The pastor recognized that Mr. A was ill, as did the majority of the congregation. There were some, however, who had difficulty grasping this idea and recognizing its full implications; these were the people who saw Mr. A as a "troublemaker" and wanted him barred from the church. The pastor found that part of his effort to help Mr. A had to be directed toward changing the attitudes of these members of the congregation.

In dealing directly with Mr. A, the pastor first took the approach of trying to reason with him and dissuade him from his false ideas. This quickly proved to be futile and led to an increase in Mr. A's accusations, both against the pastor and against other members of the congregation. On a few occasions, the pastor tried to "play along" with Mr. A, pretending to believe what he was saying. This also had no positive effect and seemed to make Mr. A more angry.

Gradually Mr. A intruded himself more and more into the pastor's private life. Letters, telegrams, and even packages from Mr. A continued to arrive at the pastor's home. Telephone calls came later and later at night. The pastor, becoming frightened, finally turned to a psychiatrist for advice.

The consulting psychiatrist agreed that Mr. A's illness made him quite difficult to deal with, but he advised the pastor to be firm and consistent. He urged the pastor not to spend time discussing Mr. A's delusions, to give a very clear message about the necessity of psychiatric treatment, and to limit Mr. A's intrusions into his private life.

A key element in this case was the fact that the pastor did not really have full confidence in the ability of the mental health system to help Mr. A. Because of this, he did not consistently follow the advice of the consultant. He wavered, at times taking a firm stand for referral, and at other times trying to deal with Mr. A's delusions himself. He was also not completely consistent in his setting of limits, partly because he was afraid of arousing Mr. A's anger. The overall result was that Mr. A's psychotic thinking and behavior continued unabated, and he showed no inclination to seek any help.

After nearly a year, an event occurred which finally brought about a resolution to this highly unstable situation. Mr. A appeared one night at the church and threw a rock through a window of the building. He then fled the scene but went immediately to the home of a relative in a nearby community. The pastor, who was in the building at the time of the incident, was not hurt, and the damage was not great, but the pastor was quite shaken. The incident made him painfully aware of the need for direct intervention, and on the advice of the psychiatric consultant, he went to the local mental health center and gave testimony to begin the process of involuntary commitment.

It is interesting that Mr. A made no attempt to resist the process of commitment. He was quite knowledgeable about the mental health system and undoubtedly knew what the consequences of his act would be. Afterward, he stayed at his relative's house for several days, and was very easily located by the authorities after the commitment was granted. It could be argued that Mr. A was indirectly asking for help all along, and after getting no consistent response, he finally took matters into his own hands and forced the pastor and the community to take action.

References for Further Reading

Bowers, Malcolm B., Jr., *Retreat from Sanity: The Structure of Emerging Psychosis*. New York: Human Sciences Press, Inc., 1974. (Paperback: Penguin, 1974)

Green, Hannah, *I Never Promised You a Rose Garden*. New York: Holt, Rinehart & Winston, 1964. (Paperback: Signet)

Kaplan, Bert, ed., *The Inner World of Mental Illness: A Series of First Person Accounts of What It Was Like*. New York: Harper & Row, Publishers, Inc., 1964.

Laing, Ronald D., *The Divided Self*. New York: Pantheon Books, Inc., 1969. (Paperback: Pelican, 1965)

 FOUR

Dealing with the Suicidal Person

Suicide is a phenomenon as old as civilization. It has been condemned by Western religions and abhorred by modern society, but it continues to occur at a disturbing rate, and there is no indication that its frequency is decreasing. This chapter will attempt to give the clergyperson a greater understanding of suicide, and it will set forth some guidelines to be used when dealing with suicidal persons.

Suicidal Gestures and Suicide Attempts

It is important to recognize, first of all, that there are two types of suicidal acts. Consider the following brief vignettes which illustrate two kinds of suicidal situations:

Case 1: A twenty-five-year-old woman has a heated argument with her husband. After the argument, she runs upstairs to the bathroom, locks herself in, opens the medicine chest, and pulls out a bottle of aspirin. She pours a dozen tablets from the bottle and swallows them. By this time her husband has run upstairs and, finding the bathroom door locked, proceeds to pound on it until he forces it open. He finds his wife lying on the floor and takes her to the hospital.

Case 2: A fifty-three-year-old businessman tells his wife that he has to go to a nearby city for two days on business. He gets into his car and drives off, but, instead of going to the city, he turns his car in the opposite direction and drives fifty miles to a small town. He checks into a motel under an assumed name, goes to his room, and locks the door. From his suitcase he takes a bottle of barbiturate sleeping pills and a bottle of whiskey. He swallows fifty of the sleeping pills and drinks the whiskey until he passes out on the floor.

It should be clear to the reader that these are two very different types of suicidal acts. The first case is an example of what is usually called a "suicidal gesture"—a self-harming act which is made with very little intent to die. The main purpose of a suicidal gesture, in most cases, is to convey a message to another person or persons. The message often has to do with anger, disappointment, or revenge, and the gesture is also a way of asking for help. These acts are usually impulsive: they are made without previous planning and often take place very soon after an intense, negative emotional experience. The suicidal gesture involves a method of self-harm which is of relatively low lethality and is done in a way which ensures that the person will be saved. In our example, the woman swallows a small amount of a relatively harmless drug, in a setting where the husband can intervene right away.

Occasionally a suicidal gesture does result in death, but this is usually due to a miscalculation, and not to a true intent to die. The person may, for example, mistakenly swallow a substance which turns out to be highly lethal, or a spouse who was expected home at a certain time may arrive several hours later. But the vast majority of these gestures do not result in death.

Our second case is very different from the first and is an example of what we shall call a true suicide attempt. In this type of suicidal act, the intent to die is quite high. The person making a true suicide attempt is also trying to convey some message to other people, but the message in these cases is clearly intended to be a final communication. The individual has relatively little expectation of survival, and this is evident from the way in which the acts are done. These attempts are carried out in a premeditated fashion, with careful planning, and they make use of methods which are highly lethal. In our example, the man takes sleeping pills and alcohol, a combination which is sure to be fatal since he has set up the situation so that he will not be found for many hours. In other true suicide attempts, the person may use such methods as shooting or jumping from a high place, methods which are obviously very lethal. These attempts are also related to traumatic life events, but the attempt may take place days, weeks, or months after the event. The individual may seem to have "gotten over" the trauma, and the suicide may come as a total surprise to family and friends.

There is an interesting and important statistical difference between suicidal gestures and true suicide attempts. In the United States, suicidal gestures are made mostly by women, while suicide attempts are made more often by men. Another way of putting this statistic is that a suicidal woman is more likely to make a gesture and be rescued, while a suicidal man is more likely to make a serious attempt that results in death. We will return to this point later in the chapter.

Table 1 summarizes the differences and contrasts between suicidal gestures and true suicide attempts.

Table 1

Comparison of Suicidal Gestures and
Suicide Attempts

Suicidal Gesture	True Suicide Attempt
Little or no intent to die	Strong intent to die
Impulsive, spur-of-the-moment	Premeditated and planned
Less lethal method	Highly lethal method
High chance of rescue	Little chance of rescue
Occurs immediately after an emotional trauma	Occurs days, weeks, or months after emotional trauma
More often done by women	More often done by men

The remainder of this chapter will deal with true suicide attempts and completed suicides, but the point must be made that suicidal gestures should never be minimized. Even though the intent to die is low in such an act, the gesture should always be taken as an indication that something is seriously wrong and that the person making the gesture needs help. The clergyperson's role in a situation where a suicidal gesture has occurred often involves working with the individual's family members, who may be so overcome with guilt, shame, or anger that they do not hear the underlying cry for help. If handled with support and acceptance, a suicidal gesture can sometimes be the beginning of a process which leads to change, growth, and the recovery of emotional health.

Mr. G was a thirty-five-year-old married man with two children. While he seemed to be successful in his profession and had no disabling emotional problems, he appeared to be constantly nervous and unable to relax. Mr. G was active in church affairs and came into frequent contact with his pastor, who noted Mr. G's ever-present anxiety. The pastor attempted a number of times to talk with Mr. G about this characteristic, but each time Mr. G would change the subject and avoid the discussion.

One morning, Mr. G's wife had difficulty rousing him, and she discovered an empty bottle of pills next to the bed. She called an ambulance and Mr. G was rushed to the hospital. In the emergency room, it was determined that the pills were a relatively mild, over-the-counter medication, and that Mr. G had actually taken only about five of them. He was admitted to the hospital for observation.

Mr. G's wife was very shaken, and she called the pastor right away. The pastor spent time with her and then went to the hospital. There he had a long talk with Mr. G, during which the subject of Mr. G's anxiety—and underlying depression—was brought out into the open for the first time.

Mr. G recovered with no medical problems and showed no suicidal thinking or intention. After his discharge from the hospital, he came to see the pastor for further counseling. He indicated that he wanted further help, and the pastor arranged a referral to a psychiatrist whom he knew personally.

Mr. G began treatment with the psychiatrist and was able to gain a greater understanding of himself and make some constructive changes in his life patterns. A year later, at the termination of his therapy, he was considerably less anxious, was finding much more enjoyment in his activities, and was relating in a more gratifying way with his family and friends. There were no further suicidal gestures.

Statistics on Suicide

Suicide is one of the ten leading causes of death in the United States, and it claims at least 25,000 lives each year. For white men between the ages of 10 and 55, suicide is the fifth highest cause of death, and for white males between 15 and 19 it is the second highest. These figures make suicide a major public health concern.

A number of statistical studies have shown correlations between suicide rates and various social and demographic factors. These results will be summarized in the following sections.

Age

The overall suicide rate increases with age and rises sharply after age forty-five. For women, the rate levels off at age seventy and then declines, but for men it continues to increase well into the eighties.

The rate of suicide in the elderly is disturbingly high, and this finding becomes even more important in light of the increasing numbers of older people in our society. In actuality, there are probably even more suicides in this age group than are reported in the statistics. People over sixty-five often have serious medical illnesses for which they must take daily medication or follow a special diet. A suicide can easily be accomplished in such a situation by the person simply not taking the medication or going off the diet. This results in a medical illness and the death is usually recorded as being a result of that illness, whereas in reality it was a suicide.

Sex

As noted above, more women make suicidal gestures, while more men make true attempts and succeed in those attempts. A suicidal man, at any age, is at a greater risk of dying than a suicidal woman.

The reason usually given for this difference is that our cultural norms and attitudes allow women to ask for help more easily than men. A man, even in our more "liberated" society, is often expected to be "strong" and to solve his problems by himself—or not to have any at all. As a result, men often conceal their difficulties and allow their level of emotional distress to rise quite high without asking for help. This ultimately can lead to a state of lonely desperation which is the setting for a suicidal act. The movement in recent years toward redefinition of sex roles will bring about a change, we hope, in this situation.

Marital Status

People who are divorced or widowed have much higher suicide rates than those who are married or single, and the rates are particularly high during the first year after divorce or bereavement. The reasons for this include the feelings of loss, grief, guilt, and anger which the divorced or widowed are likely to experience. Rates of suicide are lowest among married people, particularly if they have children.

Race

For the country as a whole, the rate of suicide among whites is greater than among blacks, but the rate is rising in the latter group. In urban areas the rates are already about equal, and in another ten years this may be true in all regions of the country. This change probably reflects a number of social, economic, and cultural factors which produce increasing stress in the black community.

Living Arrangements

Individuals living alone have a higher suicide rate than those who live with family or friends. Likewise, those people without social supports in the community—friends, family, religious group, etc.—are more prone to suicide than those with such supports.

Employment and Finances

Suicide rates are higher among the unemployed than among those who are working and are especially high in the first two months after losing a job. The presence of other financial burdens and difficulties also increases the statistical suicide risk.

Physical Illness

People who have a significant physical illness, particularly one which is disabling or very painful, have a higher rate of suicide than those who are in good physical health. If the person was very active and independent before the onset of the illness, the risk of suicide is even higher.

Alcohol Abuse

Chronic alcohol abuse is associated with an increased suicide rate, and several reasons are postulated for this finding. Alcohol is known to loosen a person's sense of perspective, thereby making problems seem even more severe than they really are. While it has a euphoric effect at first, prolonged drinking can lead to severe feelings of depression and worthlessness. In addition, alcohol can weaken the drinker's self-control and thereby trigger self-destructive acts which would otherwise not occur.

Paradoxically, an alcoholic who stops drinking is at an even higher statistical suicide risk during the first few months of abstinence than one who is drinking regularly. The cessation of drinking, while very desirable, removes the individual's major problem-solving technique and leaves the former drinker without a way to cope with painful feelings. Substitute supports and coping mechanisms must be made available at such a time if depression and suicide are to be averted.

History of Previous Attempts

It is estimated that between 50 and 80 percent of those who commit suicide have a history of at least one previous attempt.

History of Suicide in the Family

Individuals who have lost a family member through suicide show an increased rate of suicide, particularly if the individual has lost a parent in this manner. In some studies, as many as 25 percent of the persons who committed suicide were found to have a history of suicide in the immediate family.

This finding should not be interpreted to mean that a suicidal tendency is in any way inherited in the genes from one generation to the next. There is no evidence of any genetic transmission. It is felt, rather, that a family history of suicide gives an individual a "model" to imitate and acts as a constant reminder that suicide is an option.

All of these statistics have very practical significance for the professional who is faced with a potentially suicidal person. In a later section of this chapter we will consider the practical implications of these findings.

Myths About Suicide

Over the years, a number of popular misconceptions have grown up concerning suicide. These myths tend to be perpetuated in spite of overwhelming scientific evidence against them. Some of the most prevalent myths are listed and discussed in the following paragraphs.

Myth #1: People who talk about suicide never do it.

Studies have shown that 60 to 80 percent of those who talk about suicide go on to carry out their plans. A person who speaks of suicide should certainly be taken seriously.

Myth #2: Suicide occurs without any warning.

This is the companion to Myth #1 and is equally unfounded. It has been shown over and over again that the great majority of people who commit suicide have given definite warning of their intent beforehand. The warning, however, is often not heard or not taken seriously.

Myth #3: Suicidal people are always suicidal.

In every suicidal person there are fluctuations of feeling, and suicidal intent can vary markedly within the space of days or even hours. Suicidal intent occurs in relatively brief peaks, in most cases. Because of this pattern, a speedy, firm intervention with an acutely suicidal person can be very effective. The intervention does not have to solve all of the individual's problem. If it can help the person get through the next hours or days without self-harm, the suicidal feeling may pass and the person may be able to deal with the problems.

Myth #4: Suicidal people are fully intent on dying.

It has already been stated that the true suicide attempts involve a strong intent to die, but even in those cases there is some ambivalence and some faint hope of rescue. This is known from studies of people who made serious suicide attempts but survived. These people report that in the back of their minds there was a faint idea that they would be rescued and that their life situation would change.

Myth #5: Suicide occurs only among the rich (or, only among the poor).

Studies show clearly that suicide is represented at all socioeconomic levels.

Myth #6: All suicidal people have severe mental illness and are usually untreatable.

Suicidal people are obviously very unhappy and are often in great emotional conflict, but most of these people do not have chronic, severe mental illnesses. The most common psychiatric condition associated with suicide is depression, which can be treated with a high degree of success. There is not necessarily any cause for pessimism in counseling suicidal people.

Evaluating the Suicidal Person

The proper role for the clergyperson in dealing with a suicidal individual is to make a referral, but some evaluation of the seriousness of the situation must first be made. This evaluation will determine what type of referral should be made and how rapidly the referral must occur. In some cases, the individual can be given the name and phone number of a psychiatrist or clinic and encouraged to call for an appointment within a few days. In other instances, the person might need to be taken immediately to the emergency room of the nearest hospital. The following suggestions will serve as a guide in making this evaluation.

The clergyperson's first step in evaluating a suicidal person is to overcome his or her own reluctance to discuss this very uncomfortable subject. There is a widespread fear among people in general that one can "put" the idea of suicide into another person's mind by talking about it, and that the discussion of this subject will increase the likelihood of its actually happening. There is absolutely no evidence to support this idea, and, in fact, extensive experience indicates just the opposite: The more that a suicidal person is allowed to talk about the thoughts to a supportive and accepting listener, the less likely it is that the person will act on those thoughts. As one psychiatric textbook puts it:

> If the doctor can help the patient to express the same emotions in the interview that are represented by the act of suicide, the patient's own controls will be able to operate more effectively, and it may not be necessary for him to end his life.[1]

On the other hand, if the clergyperson is hesitant or embarrassed to ask about self-destructive feelings, the suicidal person will be blocked from sharing his or her most significant thoughts and wishes. This is likely to increase the person's sense of alienation and desperation and may make a suicidal act even more likely.

In the discussion with the suicidal person, the clergyperson must convey the message that he or she is committed to the preservation of life and not to the triumph of death. It is assumed throughout this chapter that this position—basically a statement of faith—is held by the clergyperson. If this commitment is in question, an entirely different set of considerations applies and this chapter is not relevant.

The clergyperson should listen carefully for clues that indicate that a troubled individual is thinking of suicide, for it will not always be immediately obvious. The presence of depression, despondency, or hopelessness is usually the first indication—although a few suicidal people may appear happy and calm. Often a hint is given in the form of a comment, such as "I don't think I can go on" or "I don't think anybody would care if I weren't here anyway." In some cases, the person will not make any comment about suicidal intent but will do some act which indicates a preparation for death, such as making a new will without any external reason for doing so, selling treasured possessions, or giving away personal property. Whenever any of these indications are seen, the clergyperson should not hesitate to take the initiative and ask about suicidal thoughts and feelings.

A very effective way to ask about these feelings is to follow what may be thought of as a hierarchy of questions, beginning with the most benign and general and proceeding to the more specific. One might start by asking the individual if he or she was ever so unhappy that it felt as though life were not worth living anymore. If this question is answered affirmatively, the next question might be whether the person had ever thought about taking his or her own life. If this is also answered affirmatively, the following questions should be explored, in order:

—How often do the thoughts occur? Are they occasional, frequent, or constant?

—Has the person thought about how he or she would actually do it?

—Is there a specific suicide plan that has been worked out in the person's mind?

—Has the person taken any steps to put the plan into action?

This line of questions should be followed in a slow, flexible manner which allows the individual to respond to each one in as much detail as is necessary. The hierarchy of questions is arranged in such a way that if a "no" response is obtained to any question, the rest of the questions need not be asked.

Table 2, which follows, is a scale for rating the severity of suicidal danger, based on the information obtained through the answers to these questions. The table rates the danger from "Grade I," the least serious, to "Grade IV," the most serious, and gives an approximate time frame for obtaining help. A person who has occasional thoughts of suicide is at a different level of risk than the person who has actually made a suicide plan. The individual who has begun to implement the plan—for example, by storing up pills or buying a gun—is the one who is most seriously at risk, and such a person may need to be hospitalized for protection.

Table 2

Gradations of Suicidal Danger

Grade	Nature of Thoughts	Time Frame for Obtaining Help
I	Occasional thoughts	within 1 week
II	Frequent thoughts	within 3 days
III	Concrete plans	immediately
IV	Plan plus implementation	immediately

During the discussion with the suicidal person, the clergyperson should also gather information about the following:

—age, marital status, employment, and financial situation

—nature of the individual's family ties, friendships, and social supports

—presence of frequent alcohol abuse or serious physical illness

—previous suicide attempts or gestures

—history of suicides in the family

This data is also crucial in determining the degree of suicidal danger. Table 3 is a list of common characteristics of people who commit suicide. The list is obtained from the statistical findings described earlier in this chapter, and it can be used as a checklist for evaluating a specific suicidal person. The more items present in any case, the higher the risk. As a rough rule of thumb, any person who is *thinking of suicide* and who has *four or more* of the characteristics in Table 3 should be considered a very serious risk and should be encouraged to seek help right away.

Table 3

Common Characteristics of Persons Who
Commit Suicide:
A Checklist

Male
White
Over 45 years of age
Living alone
Few or no family supports
Few or no close friends
Recently divorced or widowed (within 1 year)
Unemployed
Serious financial problems
Alcohol abuse
Medically ill
History of previous attempts
Family history of suicide

The Nighttime Suicidal Emergency

One of the most difficult of all mental health situations is the sudden
unexpected phone call in the middle of the night from a person on the
verge of suicide. Such calls can, of course, occur during the day as
well, but they tend to be more frequent and more difficult at night, for
several reasons. The coming of night often increases the loneliness and
desperation of the suicidal person and increases the severity of suicidal
feelings. The clergyperson is also more likely to be caught off guard
in the middle of the night, and his or her thinking may not be well-
organized. All in all, this can be an uncomfortable and upsetting experience. The clergyperson is likely to end up feeling helpless and
frustrated unless he or she has a plan ready for such occurrences
beforehand. Every clergyperson is encouraged to have such a plan
worked out, even though it will probably be used very infrequently. In
the immediate crisis, the plan can literally mean the difference between
life and death.

In setting up this plan, it is essential first of all that the clergyperson
know what emergency psychiatric facilities exist in the community and
how to contact these facilities. The emergency service of the local
Community Mental Health Center is the ideal facility; however, as
noted in chapter 2, not all communities have such centers. Private
clinics and agencies sometimes have emergency coverage, and many

psychiatrists in private practice will accept emergency calls, particularly if the psychiatrist already has a good working relationship with the clergyperson. If no other facilities exist, the emergency room of the nearest general hospital is available around-the-clock.

The suggested procedure to follow in a middle-of-the-night suicidal crisis is outlined in Figure 1, below, which is arranged in the form of a "flow sheet."

Figure 1

Flow Sheet for Nighttime Suicidal Emergencies

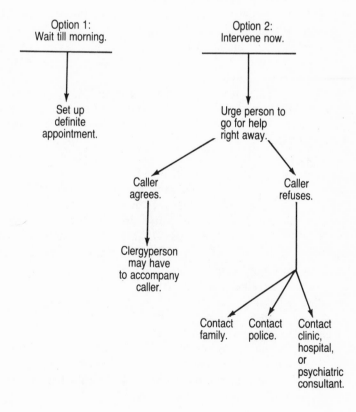

When an acutely suicidal person calls in the middle of the night, it is usually not helpful for the clergyperson to engage in a long discussion of the individual's problems over the telephone, even though the caller may want to do so. Such discussions often lead nowhere and only increase the anxiety of both parties involved. As soon as the suicidal danger is apparent, the clergyperson should pose one basic question: Can the caller wait for morning, or is it necessary to intervene right away to prevent harm? This question can sometimes be answered directly by the caller, or it may have to be arrived at from other data, particularly the factors outlined in Tables 1 and 2.

If the clergyperson has a previous relationship with the caller, and if the risk appears to be relatively low, the clergyperson may choose to delay further action until morning (Option 1, Figure 1). If that course of action is taken, a definite appointment should be set up for as early as possible the following morning. In some cases, the assurance of the clergyperson's attention the following day will be sufficient to reduce the caller's anxiety and dissipate the suicidal feelings.

If the clergyperson does not know the caller very well, or if there is any uncertainty as to the seriousness of the caller's intent, it is advised that action be taken right away (Option 2, Figure 1). The clergyperson should state clearly and simply that the person seems to need help immediately from a professional who is specially trained to deal with these problems.

It is important not to allow the suicidal person to ignore this statement or to sidetrack the discussion by bringing up various other issues. The statement may have to be repeated several times before it is heard. The clergyperson should keep in mind that the caller is caught in a deadly conflict between the self-destructive and the healthy parts of his or her personality. The individual's self-destructive tendencies will cause resistance to the clergyperson, but this resistance can be overcome by a consistent, firm, and supportive appeal to the healthier parts of the individual's personality.

The caller should be given the name and telephone number of a local psychiatric facility or a private psychiatrist and should be urged to call right away or to go to the facility. The person should be accompanied and, if no one else is available, the clergyperson may have to provide that acccompaniment. Sometimes the clergyperson's willingness to go with the suicidal person will be the key factor which motivates the caller to accept the referral. As in all situations of emotional crisis, it is important to be supportive and accepting but at the same time realistic and concerned enough to take action. In most instances, such an approach will result in the caller's accepting the referral and going for help.

If, however, the caller refuses the referral and does not show any change of mind after a reasonable period of conversation, the clergyperson is faced with the most difficult course of action. The principle here is that the clergyperson must take whatever measures are possible to avoid a suicide, even if such measures are against the caller's expressed wishes. This is the same obligation as is incumbent upon any mental health professional in a similar situation. The clergyperson is not expected to perform heroic acts or to rescue the suicidal individual single-handed. It is expected only that a reasonable effort will be made to save a life.

In practice, the "reasonable effort" which the clergyperson can make consists of contacting a third party who is in a better position to intervene—either the caller's family, the police, or a mental health agency or professional. The first choice should be to contact members of the caller's family, when this is possible. If the individual has already committed some potentially lethal suicidal act—for example, taking an overdose of medication—it may be more appropriate to contact the police who can send an ambulance. If neither the family nor police are able to intervene, the clergyperson should contact the emergency service of a local Mental Health Center, or a psychiatric consultant. These professionals can give advice on other courses of action, including involuntary commitment.

If the clergyperson chooses to follow this course of action, the caller should be told what is going to be done. If the caller objects (and this is likely to occur), the clergyperson should not abandon the plan but should state that this is part of his or her obligation to the caller, even if the caller does not like the decision. It is important to remember that the suicidal person's objections can be a way of testing the clergyperson's concern and sincerity. Standing firm in the face of such objections—while maintaining empathy at the same time—is a demonstration of concern and can have considerable therapeutic impact on the suicidal person.

The firmness of the clergyperson's position can be tempered with the assurance to the caller that the clergyperson will continue to be available and involved after the referral is made. If all of these messages are given—concern, willingness to take action, and continued availability—the caller may agree to go voluntarily for help.

In the extreme case, where the individual continues to refuse the referral, the clergyperson may have to terminate the conversation unilaterally and begin contacting the appropriate third parties. Terminating the conversation may be difficult, but to continue a fruitless discussion with a suicidal person is, in effect, to play directly into the individual's self-defeating and self-destructive patterns. Prolonged conversation wastes valuable time, increases the caller's anxiety, and conveys the message that the clergyperson is powerless to take action.

These guidelines can be applied to any situation in which the clergyperson is confronted with a suicidal person. The first course of action should always be an attempt to motivate the individual to seek help voluntarily. If this fails, however, the clergyperson must be prepared to contact the appropriate third parties, to enlist their help and advice. It is particularly important that the person's spouse (if married) or parents (if a minor) be notified when the person is suicidal and is refusing a referral. This may seem very distasteful to the clergyperson since it involves a breach of confidentiality, and the suicidal person may object to such action as well. If the clergyperson fails to do this, however, a "conspiracy of silence" will result, in which the clergyperson is forced to keep valuable information from concerned family members. If a suicidal act then occurs, the clergyperson ends up in a very uncomfortable position.

It is a principle of medical ethics that confidentiality can—and at times must—be broken in order to prevent a death from occurring.

> A physician may not reveal the confidences entrusted to him in the course of medical attendance, or the deficiencies he may observe in the character of patients, unless he is required to do so by law, or *unless it becomes necessary in order to protect the welfare of the individual* or of the community. [Emphasis mine][2]

It is reasonable to expect that the same principle should apply to members of the clergy in such situations.

Involuntary Commitment

In situations involving an acute suicidal danger, the question of involuntary commitment should always be considered. Such an action is far from ideal, but in some instances it may be the only way to avoid a suicide. The emergency commitment process has already been discussed briefly in chapter 3, and the same basic principles and procedures apply here as in the case of a psychotic person.

In many states, a person who testifies in such a proceeding must say that he or she has directly observed self-harming behavior on the part of the suicidal person. This is usually interpreted to mean that a verbal threat of suicide is not sufficient grounds for commitment; the person must have taken some tangible steps toward actually carrying out the threat. The accumulation of pills in the house, for example, or the procuring of a gun are usually considered valid grounds for a commitment petition. A physician must also testify that the suicidal individual is suffering from a mental illness; the most frequent illness diagnosed in these situations is depression.

Here again, as in the case of a psychotic individual, the clergyperson may be in a position to testify in a commitment proceeding and may sometimes be the only one in such a position. Testifying involves breaking of confidentiality and taking action against the verbalized wishes of the suicidal person, but the clergyperson should bear in mind that on some deeper level the individual may want to be rescued. If this were not true, the person would not have revealed the suicidal thoughts and acts to the clergyperson in the first place. An individual who is fully intent on dying would have no reason to reveal his or her plans to anyone.

The clergyperson's willingness to go even to this extreme degree to preserve life can have a powerful impact on a suicidal person who believes that the world no longer cares. Such an act can be the first step toward helping the person to rebuild hope and health.

References for Further Reading

Cassem, N., "Care and Management of the Suicidal Person," in *The Harvard Guide to Modern Psychiatry*, edited by Armand Nicholi. Cambridge: Harvard University Press, 1978.

MacKinnon, Roger, and Michels, Robert, *The Psychiatric Interview in Clinical Practice*. See pages 205-209—"Discussion of Suicide in the Interview." Philadelphia: W. B. Saunders Company, 1971.

Rosen, David H., "Suicide Survivors," *Western Journal of Medicine,* vol. 122 (1975), pp. 289-294.

Schneidman, Edwin S., "An Overview of Suicide," *Psychiatric Annals,* vol. 6, no. 11 (1976), pp. 606-619.

Slaby, Andrew; Lieb, J.; Tancredi, L., *Handbook of Psychiatric Emergencies,* pp. 146-152. Garden City, N.Y.: Medical Examination Publishing Co., Inc., 1975.

Zung, William W. K., "Suicide Prevention by Suicide Detection," *Psychosomatics,* vol. 20, no. 3 (1979), pp. 149-158 (with 21 references).

 FIVE

Evaluating
Depression

Of the psychiatric conditions which the clergyperson is likely to encounter, depression is by far the most common. Statistical surveys
suggest that between 20 and 30 percent of American adults develop
significant depressive symptoms at some time during their lives. It is
also believed that most of these depressed people never see a mental
health professional. Many seek help from those around them—often
from the clergy—and some receive no help at all. The ability to recognize depression in its many forms and to evaluate its severity is one
of the clergyperson's most useful tools in alleviating human suffering.

What Is Depression?

"Depression" refers to a particular way of feeling and thinking, a
certain way of behaving, and a specific set of physical and psychological
symptoms.

The depressed person has a pervasive feeling of sadness, hopelessness, and despondency. For such a person there is no joy in life,
no feeling of fulfillment, and no promise of a brighter future. The world
looks bleak, and every day is an exhausting experience. Mixed with

these feelings, the depressed individual often experiences anger and irritability, tension and nervousness. Few states of mind are as disturbing as depression.

Depressed people frequently experience what is known as "diurnal variation of mood": that is, the person's feeling state changes during the day, following a predictable pattern. Typically, the individual feels worst in the morning and has much difficulty getting out of bed and starting the day's activities. As the day wears on, the person begins to feel a bit better and by evening may feel reasonably well. The next morning, however, the cycle begins again and continues to repeat itself each day.

The depressed person also has a particular way of thinking, which has been described as a "maladaptive cognitive set." The individual's thinking seems fixed, and he or she consistently dwells on the bad side of things and never on the good. The person sees the self, the world, and the future through "glasses" which block out the positive and show only the negative. This rigid thinking style, which has received more attention in the literature in recent years,[1] is one of the major roadblocks to helping the depressed individual.

The behavior of the depressed is also characteristic. Actions are performed slowly, listlessly, and without interest. The person has trouble starting even simple tasks and often becomes inactive and withdrawn. Personal grooming and appearance are frequently neglected, and the simple basic tasks of living are left undone.

Depression affects the physiological functioning of the body in a number of ways, and the physical symptoms which result are important to recognize. There is a characteristic disturbance of *sleep,* in which the individual is able to fall asleep without much trouble, but then wakes up repeatedly during the night and has trouble getting back to sleep, finally ending up wide awake at four or five o'clock in the morning. The *appetite* is also affected in depression, with loss of interest in eating and sometimes significant weight loss. Occasionally the opposite occurs: the depressed person eats more than usual and gains considerable weight. The depressed person has trouble with *concentration* and cannot keep attention focused on matters at hand, whether they be work, reading, television, or a conversation with another person. Family and friends who do not realize that the individual is depressed sometimes become exasperated at his or her inability to pay attention to anything. Depressed people also lose interest in *sexual activity* and sometimes lose the ability to function sexually. This problem interferes with the relationship between the depressed person and the spouse, further aggravating the psychological suffering.

Depression can also manifest itself in symptoms which appear to be strictly medical. Gastrointestinal symptoms are common, including constipation, abdominal discomfort, pains in the stomach, or vague feelings of nausea. Headaches, general fatigue, lower back pains, and other uncomfortable feelings in the body often accompany depression. In some cases, a depressed individual will visit several physicians because of one or more of these physical symptoms, and the presence of depression may not be immediately evident since the person may appear superficially "happy." Closer examination, however, eventually uncovers other symptoms and feelings which lead to the correct diagnosis.

The Depressive Spectrum

Depression can express itself in a broad spectrum of severity, ranging from the mildest forms to the most disabling. Figure 1, below, is a representation of this "spectrum," along which one finds three types of depression. Each of these three entities will be discussed separately.

Figure 1
The Spectrum of Depression

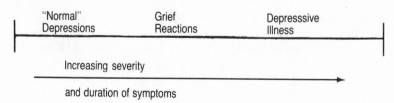

"Normal" Depressions

At one end of the depressive spectrum lie the very brief periods of despondency which are a normal part of living and which everyone experiences from time to time. These "normal depressions" occur at times of disappointment or of upsetting life events. One may experience some or all of the symptoms described above, but to a very mild degree and for no more than two or three days. These events should not be considered illnesses, but rather the human being's way of withdrawing temporarily in order to gather strength to meet a life stress.

Grief Reactions

Further along the depressive spectrum lie the grief reactions, a more severe form of depression which usually occurs after the loss of a significant person in the individual's life. Such a reaction often occurs after the death of a spouse, a parent, or a close friend, but can also occur after divorce, and has even been known to occur after the loss of a job or a home.

Grief reactions can involve any or all of the symptoms of depression described above, but in a more severe form, and of longer duration, than the "normal" depressions. An individual usually needs from three to six weeks to recover from the immediate effects of a significant loss. During that time, the person may experience sadness, hopelessness, anxiety, and irritability, along with the "maladaptive cognitive set." There may be loss of interest, loss of appetite, sleep disturbance, and any of the physical manifestations of depression. The important distinguishing characteristics of grief reactions are that they follow a real loss of an actual person or thing and that they resolve in three to six weeks. Grief reactions should not be confused with the process of mourning. The former involves specific symptoms of depression and resolves in three to six weeks; the latter involves a gradual overall reorientation to life and may take up to a year to complete.

The psychiatrist Erich Lindemann was the first to draw attention in the modern mental health literature to grief reactions as a form of depression. His paper on "Symptomatology and Management of Acute Grief"[2] was published in 1944, but it is still well worth reading for its relevance and usefulness.

Grief reactions are very often encountered by the clergy and do not usually require the intervention of a mental health professional. If the individual going through the reaction is basically healthy and has sufficient support from family and friends, he or she is usually able to recover without any permanent disability. It is important for this "grief work'' to be allowed to run its natural course. The role of the clergy-person is to provide the comfort and solace which is such an important aid to the process of healing.

Mr. and Mrs. T were both in their mid-thirties and had been married for ten years when their third child, age eighteen months, died very unexpectedly in an accident. Over the subsequent month, as the mourning process went on, both Mr. and Mrs. T developed depressive symptoms. They both experienced sleep disturbance, loss of interest in activities, and some difficulty concentrating. Mrs. T became irritable and anxious, while Mr. T became somewhat withdrawn. Both developed a disturbance of appetite, but of opposite types: Mr. T lost twelve pounds, while Mrs. T's weight increased by about the same amount. Mr. T also had a recurrence of a long-standing gastrointestinal condition which had previously been under control.

In spite of these symptoms, both Mr. and Mrs. T were able to carry on their usual activities of daily living. Mr. T returned to work after two weeks, and Mrs. T resumed her activities in the house and was able to care for the other two children. Their priest spent a good deal of time with them, as did friends and family members. The symptoms subsided after about five weeks, and the intervention of a psychiatrist was not necessary. Neither Mr. nor Mrs. T has suffered any significant depression since then.

Before leaving this subject, it should be noted that there are cases of unusually prolonged grief reactions, lasting months or even years. Individuals with these prolonged reactions do need the attention of a psychiatrist, and they should be urged to seek a consultation. In these cases, a grief reaction has precipitated a true depressive illness (see below), and professional treatment is required.

Depressive Illness

At the most severe end of the depressive spectrum lie the true depressive illnesses. In these conditions, depression is not a condition of normal living and not an understandable reaction to an actual loss, but it is an incapacitating, crippling disease. The following is illustrative:

Mrs. R was in good health until her sixties, when she began to develop arthritis, particularly affecting her hips and knees. She was a widow, lived by herself, and had no children, but had been vigorous and active in church and community functions. She had a sister who lived several blocks away, as well as a number of old friends in the neighborhood.

In her sixty-seventh year, Mrs. R underwent surgery on her hips. The surgery was successful and gave her some increased mobility, but she remained somewhat limited in her ability to get around. Soon after the surgery she began complaining of not feeling "like my old self," crying frequently, and voicing ideas of hopelessness about the future. She slept poorly, awakening frequently during the night. Her appetite decreased, and she began to lose weight. She stopped going out of the house and soon became a virtual recluse, needing to have her sister care for her night and day. She became angry and irritable with friends and very demanding of her sister.

As her symptoms worsened, Mrs. R developed the fixed idea that her illness was the result of a "mistake" that she had made a number of years earlier, which consisted of taking a shower in the home of a male relative. She dwelt on this "mistake" constantly, bringing it up in nearly every conversation. She was convinced that her present state was a result of—and a punishment for—that "mistake." Mrs. R was also convinced that her arthritis was becoming much worse, when in fact her physicians all agreed that the functioning of her legs had improved since her surgery. No amount of discussion could change her opinion.

This situation continued for nearly four months, until Mrs. R's sister could no longer care for her. At that point Mrs. R was brought to a Community Mental Health Center and treatment was begun.

In depressive illness, one may see all of the same symptoms and feelings as in other depressions, but to an even more severe degree. Here, the depressed person is so despondent that he or she is unable to function. The person may be literally unable to get out of bed. The appetite is so severely affected that malnutrition can result. Sleep is severely disturbed, and concentration is impossible. As the illness progresses and the symptoms increase, suicidal thinking can occur, and suicidal acts are not uncommon in this disease.

In depressive illness, the maladaptive cognitive set is so marked that the individual may actually become delusional, that is, may develop false ideas which are not logical and do not fit the cultural beliefs of the individual, yet are fixed and cannot be changed by rational discussion. The delusions of a depressed person often involve guilt or a feeling of being an extremely evil person. As in our case example, an individual may believe that he or she has committed unforgiveable sins in the past and that the depression is a punishment for those sins. The person may also be convinced that the disease is incurable and will result in death. Because of these fixed ideas, many seriously depressed people are very pessimistic about the efficacy of psychiatric treatment and may even refuse it outright.

In depressive illness there may also develop what are known as "somatic delusions"—false, fixed ideas regarding the body and what is happening to it. The depressed person may believe that his or her body is rotting away, falling to pieces, or turning to stone. These delusions can sometimes be quite bizarre. One severely depressed man, for example, believed that there was a snake in his stomach which was devouring his intestines. These delusional ideas can be understood by an outside observer as metaphoric expressions of how the depressed individual feels. The problem in dealing with delusional depressed people is, however, that they themselves do not think of the statements as metaphors, but are convinced of their reality.

It is worthless for the clergyperson to attempt to persuade a delusional, depressed person that his or her ideas are not correct. As with the psychotic person (see chapter 3), such debate will only widen the gap between the depressed individual and the clergyperson. It is also not very useful to discuss these delusional ideas from the theological point of view—in terms of sin, divine punishment, etc. What is usually most helpful is to treat the delusion as a metaphor, ignoring the literal content of the statement and responding instead to the feeling that lies behind it.

The onset and course of depressive illness are quite different from that of the grief reactions. The illness may sometimes occur after a significant loss of an actual person, but in many cases it begins without an obvious major loss having occurred. One usually can identify retrospectively an upsetting event which seemed to trigger the illness, but the severity of the depression is often far out of proportion to the severity of the precipitating event. In some instances, as with Mrs. R, the depression may follow what appears to be a positive event. In depressive illness, it is believed that the individual probably has a biochemical abnormality of the brain which predisposes him or her to major depressions, even in response to life events which do not appear to an outsider to be overwhelming. The interplay of life events and brain biochemistry is very complex and is not completely understood at this time.

As for duration, the depressive illnesses last much longer than the grief reactions. If not treated, a depressive illness can last anywhere from six to nine months. It is believed that every depression will eventually resolve spontaneously, but one cannot wait for this to occur. The risks of malnutrition and suicide are high, and a state of chronic invalidism can result if the disease is not treated promptly.

Rating the Severity of Depression

We have presented "normal" depressions, grief reactions, and depressive illness as three distinct entities, but in reality they shade into each other along a continuum. Within each group as well, there are many gradations of severity. In an attempt to measure the severity of depressions, some researchers have developed rating scales in which severity can be expressed in the form of a numerical score. One of these is the Zung Self-Rating Depression Scale, developed by the psychiatrist Dr. William Zung in 1965. (See Figure 2.) The Zung scale consists of twenty statements; the depressed person responds to each statement by checking one of the four boxes, indicating to what degree it applies to him or her. A numerical score—from one to four—is given for each statement, dependent on which box is checked. The scores are added together and the total score for all 20 items becomes the significant index of depression. A person indicating no symptoms at all would receive a score of 25. Scores between 26 and 49 are considered "normal" (what we have called "normal" depression); from 50 to 59, "mild depression"; from 60 to 69, "marked depression"; and above 70 indicates "severe depression." The Zung Scale is widely used for research purposes and is also used by some clinics as part of the evaluation of depressed patients.

Most mental health professionals, however, do not use a formal test to determine the severity of depression. A very adequate assessment usually can be made simply by asking appropriate questions and listening carefully to the answers. The clergyperson should also know how to

Figure 2

The Zung Self-Rating Depression Scale[3]

	A Little of the Time	Some of the Time	Good Part of the Time	Most of the Time
1. I feel down hearted, blue and sad				
2. Morning is when I feel the best				
3. I have crying spells or feel like it				
4. I have trouble sleeping through the night				
5. I eat as much as I used to				
6. I enjoy looking at, talking to and being with attractive women/men				
7. I notice that I am losing weight				
8. I have trouble with constipation				
9. My heart beats faster than usual				
10. I get tired for no reason				
11. My mind is as clear as it used to be				
12. I find it easy to do the things I used to				
13. I am restless and can't keep still				
14. I feel hopeful about the future				
15. I am more irritable than usual				
16. I find it easy to make decisions				
17. I feel that I am useful and needed				
18. My life is pretty full				
19. I feel that others would be better off if I were dead				
20. I still enjoy the things I used to do				

make such an assessment, for it has very practical implications. As indicated by Figure 3, the more severe the degree of depression, the more likely it is that medication and/or hospitalization will be necessary in addition to counseling. Individuals whose depressions lie on the more severe side of the spectrum should therefore be referred to a psychiatrist or psychiatric clinic, at least for an evaluation.

The next section of this chapter will deal with the clergyperson's evaluation of the depressed individual; following that, a final section will discuss some aspects of the psychiatric treatment of depression.

Figure 3

The Spectrum of Depression, with Implications
for Treatment

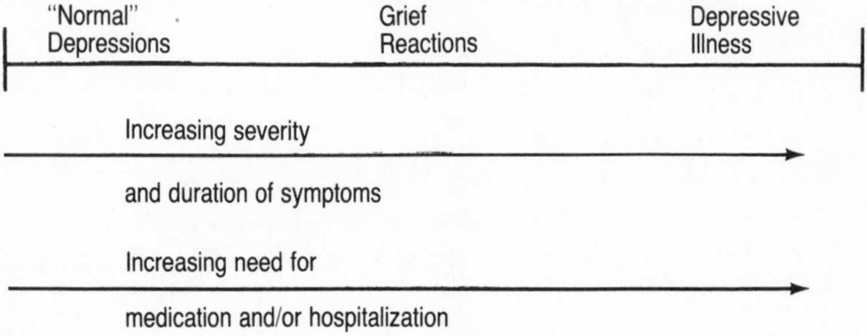

"Normal" Depressions	Grief Reactions	Depressive Illness

Increasing severity
⟶
and duration of symptoms

Increasing need for
⟶
medication and/or hospitalization

Evaluating the Depressed Person

As noted above, the evaluation of a depressed person is largely a matter of asking the proper questions, most of which are quite simple and straightforward. Table 1 is a checklist which can be used by the clergyperson as a guide in gathering information which can then be used to make a rough determination of the severity of depression. The list can also be used to organize the data for presentation to a psychiatric consultant. The sections of the checklist will be discussed in order.

Psychiatric Symptoms

These psychological symptoms have been described above, but several items warrant comment here. "Psychomotor retardation" refers to a significant slowing down of the individual's actions and speech and has nothing to do with "mental retardation." "Diurnal variation," as noted, is the pattern of mood changes as the day progresses, going from most depressed in the morning to least depressed at night.

It is useful to look for all of these features in every person who comes for help with emotional problems. An individual's mood may appear superficially normal; yet closer examination may reveal some or all of the other symptoms listed here. These cases are the so-called "smiling depressions," which are often missed, even by trained professionals.

Physical Symptoms

These are symptoms of depression which are more physical in nature, rather than psychological. A wide variety of such symptoms have been reported, and the checklist mentions those which are most frequently found. Depression can bring on new physical complaints and can also worsen already existing illnesses. (This point will be elaborated further in chapter 8.)

Duration

In evaluating a depressed person, the clergyperson should always determine approximately when the present symptoms began. Grief reactions, as discussed above, usually resolve in three to six weeks; any depression of longer duration is probably a depressive illness.

Precipitants

Every depressed person should be asked about stressful life events in the weeks or months preceding the onset of the depression. Even if the individual is unable to report any events, the clergyperson should listen carefully for clues to their existence. Depression often interferes with the clarity of the individual's memory, and a bit of detective work may be called for. The identification of precipitants is important because the prognosis is much better when one can be found. Those depressions where no precipitating cause can be found tend to be more difficult to treat and more likely to recur.

The most frequently found precipitants to depression are losses of important persons or objects. Life changes—retirement, marriage of children, job change, etc.—can also precipitate depression, as can physical illness, particularly when it involves disability for prolonged periods of time.

Table 1

Checklist for the Evaluation
of Depression

I. Psychiatric Symptoms

Mood of sadness, hopelessness, despair
Irritability, anger
Loss of appetite (or overeating)
Weight loss (or weight gain)
Sleep disturbance
Difficulty concentrating
Decreased interest in activities
Decreased sexual interest
Psychomotor retardation
Delusional ideas:
   Delusions of guilt
   Somatic delusions
Suicidal thinking
Diurnal variation

II. Physical Symptoms

Gastrointestinal problems (ulcers, abdominal pain, etc.)
Headaches
Fatigue, washed-out feeling
Pain anywhere in the body
Worsening of an already existing illness

III. Duration

IV. Precipitating Events

V. Previous Depressions

Symptoms
Duration
Treatment

Previous Depressions

It is important to ask every depressed person about past depressions, including symptoms, duration, and treatment (if any). This data is very useful in determining how to deal with the present depression. Any person with a history of one or more depressions in the past should have a psychiatric consultation and may need ongoing psychiatric treat-ment. An individual who responded well to medication during a past depression probably will do so again and should be encouraged to accept it. On the other hand, one who has had an unpleasant experience with psychiatric treatment during a past depression is likely to resist a referral, and the clergyperson may have to work hard to overcome that resistance. Finally, the duration of the present depression can sometimes be predicted from the duration of past episodes.

Once the clergyperson has accumulated this information, it can be used to determine whether or not a referral should be made. The ideal individual for the clergyperson to counsel alone would be one who has a depression of mild degree and short duration (less than six weeks) with a clear precipitating event and no history of depressions in the past. The symptoms should not be incapacitating, and there should be no suicidal thinking. When more serious symptoms are present—marked weight loss, suicidal thinking, delusions, inability to work, etc.—the clergyperson should think in terms of referral.

When a psychiatric referral or consultation is arranged (see chapter 2), the clergyperson can use the checklist (Table 1) to organize the data for presentation to the psychiatric consultant. The checklist contains all the essential information which the consultant will need to know, and much time can be saved if the clergyperson simply reads down the list and gives the pertinent facts. The consultant will appreciate the or-ganization of the data, and the working relationship between the two professionals will be simplified and enhanced.

The Psychiatric Treatment of Depression

In past years, depression was often a very incapacitating illness and at times was fatal, either through suicide or through the individual's persistent failure to eat. Until about thirty-five years ago, depressed people usually had to be treated in hospitals, under close surveillance. The disease was progressive; the treatment was long; and the results were often discouraging.[4] In the past quarter-century, however, some very effective medications have been developed for treatment of depres-sion, and our understanding of the psychological dynamics of depression has been greatly increased. As a result, the rate of success in treating depression has risen, and most depressed people today are treated as outpatients.

Medication

The general public is often fearful of psychiatric medications. Even the mention of the subject usually evokes fears of being "drugged," "doped up," feeling drowsy all the time, and being unable to function or think clearly. Some of these effects do occur when the medication is used *incorrectly*, and an important part of a psychiatrist's function is to watch carefully for these side effects and to make appropriate changes if they occur. When used properly and in the correct dosage, the medicines for depression do not interfere with functioning, cloud the individual's thinking, or cause drowsiness. In fact, patients usually report that they can function much more effectively and think more clearly after they have begun taking the medication.

It is important for the clergy—and the public at large—to know that there are nearly a dozen different medications on the market in this country for depression, and that psychiatrists do not know in advance which depressed person will be helped by which drug. It is sometimes necessary to try two or three different medications before finding the one which works best. One of the psychiatrist's most difficult tasks in treating depression is keeping the patient motivated and interested enough to stick with the treatment until the right medication is found. This may take several weeks.

The clergyperson can be very helpful in this regard by encouraging the depressed individual not to give up the treatment if results are not obtained right away. In the great majority of cases, an effective medication is eventually found. This trial-and-error procedure is far from ideal, but in the present state of psychiatric knowledge, there is no other method.

Hospitalization

If a depression is particularly severe, hospital admission may be necessary to prevent suicide or to make sure that adequate nutrition is maintained. It may also be necessary when the depressed person is so withdrawn that it would be very difficult to bring him or her for outpatient treatment, or when delusions or agitation make it impossible for the person to be managed at home. Hospital stays for depression in most cases last from two to four weeks.

The basic purpose of the hospitalization is to provide supervision and nutrition, to prevent suicide, and to find the best medication. The hospital stay is also an opportunity for the psychiatrist and the other hospital staff to get to know the family of the depressed individual. It is now standard practice in many hospitals for the family to be asked to come for at least one evaluation session. The clergyperson can help the treatment process by encouraging the family to come for these sessions. The value of this family approach has become more and more evident in the past two decades. Depressed individuals are often reacting to problems in the family, and in some cases the depression will not lift until the family problem has been adequately resolved. On the other hand, the depression can also create family problems, which must also be dealt with. Depression, like many other mental illnesses, is in large part a family disease.

More and more psychiatric hospitals are recognizing the importance of the clergy, both as valuable sources of information about patients and their families, and as partners in the overall treatment process. A clergyperson who is willing to help in the treatment of a hospitalized parishioner and his or her family should feel free to take the initiative and contact the hospital or the treating psychiatrist.

Psychotherapy

Every depressed person in psychiatric treatment—whether inpatient or outpatient—participates in some form of psychotherapy. (See chapter 9.) In some cases, this consists of relatively brief sessions which focus on how to cope with present-day problems of living. In others, the psychotherapy is more intensive, with longer and more frequent sessions, in which the therapist and the patient try to understand the emotional roots and causes of the depression. Group therapy may also be a part of the treatment, and sometimes the spouse is involved in joint therapy sessions. The psychiatrist and other mental health professionals involved in the treatment will design a treatment plan to fit the problems, needs, and abilities of each depressed individual. Psychiatric treatment involves much more than the dispensing of medication, although many of the lay public do not know this.

Electroconvulsive Therapy

Electroconvulsive therapy—often incorrectly referred to as "shock therapy"—is a form of treatment for depression. Of all the different types of treatment in psychiatry, this one is the most frightening to the general public, and the most overlaid with misconceptions.

The development of electroconvulsive therapy (ECT) began in the early 1900s when it was noticed that depressed epileptics showed remarkable lessening of their depressions after an epileptic seizure. The seizure itself seemed to have an anti-depression effect. From this chance observation, physicians came upon the idea of deliberately inducing a seizure in order to combat depression. The idea was tested carefully, and the method was found to be very effective.

During the ECT treatment, a minute current of electricity is passed across the skull, setting off a generalized seizure which lasts about twenty seconds. Shortly before the procedure the patient is given a drug which causes several minutes of unconsciousness, and the patient therefore feels no pain or discomfort whatever during the seizure. The treatment is closely supervised by a physician.

The main advantage of ECT is that it works very rapidly, as opposed to medications, which may take several weeks to produce any effect. The results of ECT are quite dramatic: improvement in mood and other symptoms can occur within hours after the first few treatments. This therapy is therefore most useful when depressive symptoms are life-threatening and relief must be immediate. In some cases ECT can literally be life saving.

Those who oppose the use of ECT argue that it causes permanent brain damage. This has never been proved conclusively to be true, but even the possibility of permanent damage makes most psychiatrists hesitate to use this treatment. In practice, medication is always tried first. A large percentage of depressed individuals respond very well to the medications, and in only a very small number of cases is ECT even considered.

At times in the past, ECT was used incorrectly. These abuses have been recognized, and psychiatrists are now much more careful about its use. Most psychiatric hospitals have rather elaborate procedures to ensure that the treatment is justified and that the patient is given all the information necessary to make an informed decision. Except in very extraordinary circumstances, ECT cannot be used without the patient's consent. Most hospitals in fact require that consent be obtained not only from the patient, but from another member of the patient's family as well. In some states, it is even necessary to get approval of a special board of experts before ECT can be done.

When ECT is proposed, the patient always has the right to know why this treatment is being suggested and what risks and benefits are to be expected. The clergyperson counseling a depressed individual who has been advised to have ECT can be most helpful by encouraging a calm, rational approach and by aiding the patient and the family in obtaining information.

Involuntary Commitment

The question of involuntary commitment to a psychiatric hospital occasionally arises in the case of a depressed person. This step may be necessary if the individual is refusing treatment and is so depressed that he or she is in danger of becoming physically ill or of dying. All of the same considerations apply here as in other instances of involuntary commitment. (See chapters 3 and 4.) Each state has its own laws and procedures regarding involuntary commitment, and the clergyperson is advised to find out what the procedures are in his or her locality. Here again, the clergyperson may be faced with the possibility of testifying in a commitment proceeding, and the choice can sometimes be a difficult one. Hospitalization may be distasteful, but it is often lifesaving in this potentially fatal illness.

References for Further Reading

Goodwin, Frederick K., and Bunney, William E., Jr., "A Psychological Approach to Affective Illness," *Psychiatric Annals,* vol. 3, no. 2 (1973), pp. 19-53.

Klerman, G., "Affective Disorders," in *The Harvard Guide to Modern Psychiatry,* edited by Armand Nicholi, pp. 253-281. Cambridge: Harvard University Press, 1978.

Kaplan, Bert, ed., *The Inner World of Mental Illness.* New York: Harper & Row, Publishers, Inc., 1964. This is a collection of firsthand accounts of the experience of severe mental illness, including several striking descriptions of depression.

 SIX

Substance Abuse: Drugs and Alcohol

It is estimated that in this country nearly ten million people have serious problems of alcohol dependence, and that between two and four million individuals are using drugs in some way injurious to their health. These figures probably underestimate the true magnitude of the problem since many cases of drug and alcohol abuse go undetected and untreated. It was once believed that these problems existed mainly among men, and primarily in the working-class and underprivileged segments of our population. We now know that the problems are widespread at all levels of our society, affecting women as well as men, the well-to-do along with the poor, the suburbs and towns as well as the inner cities. Particularly disturbing is the increasing use of drugs and alcohol among young people of high school age, and even of elementary school age.

This chapter will not deal with the specific characteristics of the excessive use of alcohol and the various drugs, but instead will focus on those psychological features which are common to all forms of substance abuse. (Specific information on the properties and effects of alcohol and different drugs may be found in the references at the end of this chapter.) An understanding of these underlying features will enable the clergyperson to make more effective interventions and referrals in dealing with these problems.

The Concept of Substance Abuse

It has become a common practice in the mental health field to use the term "substance abuse" rather than "drug and alcohol abuse." This is an important concept because it implies that *any* substance which can be taken into the body can be abused, that is, can be used excessively, or in ways which are harmful. This is true not only of drugs and alcohol, but also of food, vitamins, aspirin tablets, or laxatives. This broad view is useful since the clergyperson is likely to see many different forms of substance abuse.

Table 1 presents a list of substances which are frequently abused. The reader will no doubt be quick to see the marked differences between the items on this list. Some substances are available in any supermarket or drugstore; others can be obtained only through illegal and dangerous means. Some are drugs which are used for legitimate purposes in medicine, while others have no legitimate use whatever. Some exert their ill effects slowly, over long periods of time, while a single dose of some others can be extremely harmful or even fatal. But while the particular substances may vary from case to case, substance abuse always has the same basic psychological characteristics and dynamics. It is to these features that we will now turn our attention.

The Statements of Substance Abuse

The substance abuser can be thought of as making several "statements" about his or her basic style of coping with stress. These statements are rarely voiced explicitly, but they are evident in the abuser's patterns of behavior over long periods of time.
Statement 1: "When I feel bad, I put something into myself and that makes me feel better."

This sums up one of the key defense mechanisms of the substance abuser. The abuser does not think seriously or deeply about problems, does not meet stresses by taking definitive action to change the environment, and does not turn to others for help. Instead, he or she takes a passive position, letting the substance do all the work. There is an almost magical quality in this way of coping: the substance is expected to remove all anxiety and solve all problems. From a developmental

Table 1

Substances Which Are Commonly Abused
(with common street names)

Food
Alcohol
Glue and other volatile solvents
Household medicines
      aspirin
      vitamins
      laxatives
Barbiturate sleeping pills ("downers")
      phenobarbital
      Nembutal ("yellow jackets," "yellows")
      Seconal ("red devils," "reds")
      Tuinal ("reds and blues," "Tooies")
Other sleeping pills
      Quaalude ("Ludes")
      Noludar
      Doriden
      Placidyl
Marijuana ("pot," "grass," "tea," "hash")
Narcotic drugs
      heroin
      Dilaudid
      codeine
      methadone
      Demerol
Cocaine ("coke")
Amphetamine drugs ("uppers")
      Methedrine ("speed," "monster")
      Dexedrine
      diet pills
Hallucinogens
      Lysergic Acid (LSD, "acid")
      Phencyclidine (PCP, "angel dust")

point of view this attitude is reminiscent of the infant, whose hunger and tension are relieved by the "magical" milk which satisfies and removes all unpleasant feelings. This is not to say that substance abusers consistently function on this infantile level; they may behave maturely and effectively for long periods of time, but under stress they frequently revert to this very primitive manner of coping.

Mr. B first entered a psychiatric hospital at age thirty. He was single and unemployed at the time, and he stated that he had come to the hospital to get help in stopping his use of drugs. He gave a history of substance abuse going back more than twenty years. At different times, he had been a heavy eater, a heavy smoker of marijuana, and a heavy drinker. In his early twenties he experimented with LSD, barbiturates, and heroin. At age twenty-eight he began using methedrine and continued using it until shortly before his admission to the hospital.

Mr. B described the feeling state produced by methedrine as follows: "You feel really great. There is a physical feeling of being lifted up, and you feel like you can do anything."

In the course of giving his history, Mr. B spoke of a blanket which he had as a very young child. He described his attachment to this blanket and how he would frequently suck and chew on it. He went on to say that he slept with the blanket throughout his childhood and most of his adolescence, and that, when it finally disintegrated, he saved a small piece of it and carried it around in his wallet for many years.

Statement 2: "When I put the substance into myself, I feel satiated and I don't have to think about what is troubling me."

A major function of substance abuse, regardless of the nature of the substance, is the avoidance of painful thoughts and feelings. The exact nature of the feelings will vary from one individual to the next; what is unbearable for one person may not be so for the next.

Mr. G (introduced in chapter 4) had for approximately four years taken sleeping pills every night. The medication was addicting and dangerous, and Mr. G was taking it without the knowledge of his physician. He was fully aware of the risks he was taking, but he could not be without his pills.

The sleeping medication was part of a larger pattern of keeping unpleasant feelings out of awareness. As Mr. G put it during his psychotherapy: "I had to be busy all of the time and never let myself think about what I was feeling. At night I had to take medicine so that I would fall asleep immediately. I couldn't let myself lie awake even for a minute."

Mr. G had suffered severe traumas in childhood, including the death of one of his parents. The feelings which he worked so hard to keep out of awareness were those of deep sadness and depression, as well as intense anger.

The concept of "reinforcement" is useful in understanding substance abuse. Every time the abuser uses a substance to avoid an unpleasant feeling or thought, the behavior is reinforced—the abuser is *rewarded* by not having to face something painful. These rewards quickly enhance and solidify the patterns of behavior, so that the substance abuse becomes very difficult to change. We may state the same problem a different way by saying that every time the abuser runs away from unpleasant feelings, he or she becomes less used to looking at those feelings and therefore more frightened of them. The longer the abuse goes on, the more afraid the abuser is of giving it up.

Statement 3: "I may not like the substance I use, but I can't do without it."

One should not assume that the substance user always enjoys the abuse behavior, for in many cases he or she does not. Without the substance, however, the abuser would be far more uncomfortable. The individual strikes an unconscious bargain, settling for the lesser discomfort in place of the greater.

> Mrs. K was a thirty-three-year-old married woman who sought treatment because of depression of about six months' duration. She was significantly overweight and reported that she had gained forty-five pounds since the onset of the depression. She then revealed a long history of weight fluctuations since her early teens, with eating "rampages" alternating with periods of intense dieting. As Mrs. K's therapy progressed, it became clear that there was a close correlation between overeating and certain unpleasant painful feelings. Mrs. K came to see that her eating binges were unconsciously designed to keep these feelings out of awareness.
>
> It was significant that Mrs. K never really enjoyed eating. During her periods of overeating, she reported feeling a deep sense of disgust and self-loathing, but was unable to control her behavior. Many months of treatment passed before Mrs. K could finally make a permanent change in her eating behavior.

Social and Interpersonal Features of Substance Abuse

A very important aspect of substance abuse is its social and interpersonal dimension. Many forms of substance abuse, first of all, create a social bond between fellow abusers. This is perhaps most obvious among alcoholics who drink together and certain drug abusers who come together to take their drugs. Some substance abusers' only significant social contacts are built around the abuse behavior. These individuals often have severe deficits in the ability to relate to others, and the abuse behavior sometimes gives them the only framework they have for making contacts with other human beings.[1]

Substance abuse can also be a way of exerting control over other people, particularly other family members. Through his or her behavior, the abuser can exercise a great deal of power—albeit in a self-defeating way—over the rest of the family. Plans may be disrupted; decisions may be undermined; and the entire functioning of the family can be brought to a halt because of the abuser's actions. To illustrate this, one need only think of how much disruption is caused in a family when one of the parents disappears on a drinking spree.

On a more subtle level, the abuser may even control which subjects can and cannot be discussed in conversation. (See the next case.) This kind of controlling behavior often makes the other family members feel quite angry; at the same time, however, they are blocked from taking action or ventilating their feelings because they feel that the abuser is "sick" and therefore not responsible for his or her actions. The family's frustration can build up, sometimes to dangerous levels, and quarreling or even overt violence can result. In some cases, the family's anger is expressed in other ways, as in the following example.

Mrs. J was a thirty-four-year-old housewife with two children. She came for psychiatric treatment after a suicide attempt by drug overdose. She had a long history of depression and had made several other suicide attempts in the past. Many family problems became evident during her treatment, so much so that most of the treatment was carried out through family therapy sessions. A major family problem was the relationship between Mrs. J and her seventeen-year-old daughter; the two regarded each other with hostility and overt jealousy.

As the therapy progressed, it was noted that Mrs. J would periodically take "a little too much" of her medication and would appear drowsy. The medication was prescribed for a chronic medical illness which Mrs. J had had for many years. The reason for this abuse of medication did not become clear until many weeks of therapy had passed. Mrs. J's overdosing followed arguments with her daughter, particularly when the daughter tried to point out irritating things that Mrs. J was doing. The medication abuse also followed arguments with Mrs. J's husband, in which the husband sided with the daughter.

In effect, Mrs. J was saying to her family that she would tolerate no criticism and no discussion of her role in the family's difficulties. Her overdosing invariably disrupted family plans and caused anxiety for all concerned. It was also an obvious threat of what she might do in the future. The medication, it should be noted, was essential for treatment of her medical condition and therefore could not be stopped.

The degree of the family's anger at Mrs. J became evident when she finally did take a large overdose at home. The family members, who were at home at the time, did not take any action right away. Instead, they waited for nearly four hours to see "if she would wake up by herself." Because of this delay, Mrs. J came very close to dying.

Another aspect of substance abuse is that, while it provides an escape from some feelings, it allows for the expression of many others which would usually be held back by inhibition or embarrassment. The intoxicated state allows the individual to express powerful emotions— often of anger and hostility, but sometimes of affection or sexuality— and later disclaim all responsibility for those feelings. ("I didn't mean anything I said—I was drunk!") This phenomenon is neither deliberate nor fully conscious, but it occurs nonetheless, and the gratification obtained is another powerful reinforcer of substance abuse.

A thirty-nine-year-old married man, Mr. W, was admitted to a psychiatric ward of a general hospital after he had stabbed his wife and then stabbed himself in the neck. His past history revealed that he had been a heavy drinker for many years and also had a record of several arrests for assaultive behavior. When sober, he was mild-mannered, quiet, and rather shy; when intoxicated with alcohol, he frequently became angry and violent. All of his arrests had, in fact, occurred while he was drunk.

This pattern was repeated in the hospital. On admission, Mr. W was agitated, disheveled, and had a strong smell of alcohol on his breath. Two days later, he was well groomed, neatly dressed, pleasant, and cooperative. He had no memory of stabbing either his wife or himself. (His acts had been observed and confirmed by several witnesses.)

This aspect of substance abuse is quite important to recognize when one is dealing therapeutically with an abuser. One of the main goals of treatment with such a person is to find a way for him or her to express these blocked-off feelings without the use of drugs or alcohol. Once this can be accomplished, the need for the drug or alcohol often begins to diminish.

One final interpersonal aspect of substance abuse is that the abuser may be covertly aided and encouraged by other people, particularly family members. In a family with a father who drinks, for example, the family members may all express great concern about the problem and may all claim that they want to help the father stop drinking. At the same time, however, bottles of liquor may be left in the house, and drinks may be served before dinner. Similarly, in a family with a teenage drug user, the parents may look the other way as the child smokes marijuana in the bedroom. Here again, this behavior is not deliberate and the family members may not even be fully conscious of their actions.

Intensive studies of families of substance abusers have shown that, in many cases, the abuser is serving an important psychological function in the family's overall dynamics. For this reason, every family member has an investment in keeping the abuse behavior going. One frequent finding is that the parents of the abuser have a disturbed relationship with each other, and the abuser's behavior allows them to cover up these deficiencies. John Schwartzman studied a sample of twenty-one families, each of which included at least one male heroin or barbiturate addict. The author states:

> The marital dyad in these families was characterized by emotional distance and a lack of interaction—except for those periods when the addict seemed to need the most help, i.e., when he was using drugs or his parents thought he was using drugs. The mutually accepted belief that the addict is unable to resist drugs functioned to make his parents interact, if only to argue about him.[2]

One may also find in these families difficult relationships between the parents and the children. As soon as one child begins to abuse drugs or alcohol, the other children feel a sense of relief that the parents' attention is no longer focused on them. This leads the siblings to support, in covert ways, the behavior of the abuser.

In short, substance abuse can cover over a multitude of family problems, and for that reason it may be covertly encouraged for long periods of time. A corollary to this is that when the substance abuse is controlled through successful treatment, a number of other problems in the abuser's family may suddenly be revealed. Because of this, families sometimes resist the idea of treatment for the abuser and may remove the individual from treatment just when progress is beginning to occur.

The interpersonal aspect of alcohol abuse has been explored most fully by the proponents of Transactional Analysis. Acccording to Eric Berne, alcoholism is not a "disease," but rather a "life game," which has definite rules, players, a "script," and a "payoff," or reward, for the alcoholic.[3] Claude Steiner has expanded Berne's ideas and added his own concepts of the dynamics of alcoholism.[4] Most psychiatrists would disagree with Berne's assertion that alcoholism is not an illness, but virtually all would agree that his interpersonal analysis of the "game" is very useful in understanding and treating abusers of alcohol.

General Guidelines for Dealing with the Substance Abuser

Individuals often will not reveal a substance abuse problem directly, but instead will hint at it or let the secret slip in the course of talking about something else. It is important that the clergyperson overcome the constraints of embarrassment and polite conversation and pursue these hints when they are given. Timing and tact are important, but eventually direct questions should be asked.

Establishing trust with substance abusers may be quite difficult. These individuals often come from family settings in which they were not able to trust their parents and siblings, and this mistrust carries over to all other significant relationships. The clergyperson must encourage self-disclosure and demonstrate a nonjudgmental attitude regarding the substance abuse. Acts which are illegal or very dangerous should never be encouraged, but by the same token they should never be condemned. Discussion, exploration, and understanding will ultimately be more effective than judgment or punishment.

Confidentiality may become an important issue in dealing with substance abusers, particularly with adolescents whose parents are not aware of the abuse behavior. If the abuser is in danger of immediate physical harm, for example, from withdrawal effects or a drug overdose, it may be necessary to break confidentiality. This may also be necessary if the abuser states clearly that he or she is about to commit a crime or harm another person. In most cases, however, these situations are not likely to arise, and the clergyperson can agree to keep information secret for a limited period of time. The ultimate goal should always be to help the abuser to gather the courage to disclose the secret, accept responsibility for it, and seek professional help.

It is essential that the clergyperson recognize and acknowledge the emotional distress which underlies all forms of substance abuse. All too often, individuals become frustrated, angry, and critical toward substance abusers, losing sight of the stress and pain which lie behind the behavior. One reason for this reaction is that substance abuse is frequently thought of by the general public as self-induced and deliberate. Many people assume that abusers of drugs and alcohol could stop their behavior easily if they just had enough willpower, motivation, or moral fiber. It is only recently that the lay public has begun to understand that these conditions are illnesses, which are self-perpetuating and very difficult to cure. The substance abuser should no more be blamed for his or her illness than should an individual with pneumonia or cancer. On the other hand, the abuser is not completely free of responsibility; he or she is not expected to stop the disease single-handedly but *is* expected to seek the help of others with whose assistance the sickness can be arrested.

Some Questions for Evaluating Substance Abuse

One of the best ways in which the clergyperson can demonstrate concern and understanding for the substance abuser is by asking pertinent questions and listening carefully to the answers. The data which is elicited by these questions will help the clergyperson to understand the abuser and will also help determine what kind of referral should be made, and how quickly this referral needs to be done. The questions which follow on page 99 are based on an understanding of those basic psychological principles of substance abuse which were discussed earlier in this chapter.

What does the substance do for you when you take it?

The clergyperson should try to elicit a description of the feeling state which is produced by the substance. One should never assume that a substance has the same effect on everyone; each person reacts differently, depending on genetic predisposition, personality, past experience, and the setting in which the abuse takes place. In addition, the clergyperson should try to elucidate the feeling state which the substance helps the abuser to *avoid*. Here again, this may vary greatly from one individual to the next.

In what circumstances do you take the substance?

The clergyperson should listen carefully to identify the stresses to which the individual is reacting, and what types of difficulties are being avoided. In most cases, the pattern of abuse will not be random but will be related to negative life events or upsetting interpersonal experiences. It is sometimes useful to have the individual describe in detail the events leading up to the most recent episode of substance abuse. This can sometimes reveal stresses and feelings of which the person was previously unaware.

How do the people around you react to the substance abuse?

The answer to this question may reveal that family or friends are covertly supporting the abuse behavior and will also show what role the abuser is playing in the family or social group. If this line of questioning uncovers significant family problems, the treatment will probably have to involve the entire family, at least to some degree.

When, and under what circumstances, did the abuse start?

It is often fruitful to ask the substance abuser to describe the first episode of abuse behavior and the events surrounding it. This history can yield some important insights into the individual's underlying emotional dynamics.

Have you ever tried to stop?

This simple question can uncover a great deal of useful information. Many substance abusers will report that they have stopped their abuse behavior at times in the past, but then relapsed. If this is the case, it is important to find out whether the person stopped the behavior alone or with professional help. How long was the abstinence maintained, and what stresses seemed to cause the relapse? This information is very useful in making a referral. An individual with whom one agency or type of treatment was successful in the past should probably be encouraged to go back to the same agency or treatment. Likewise, the negative treatment experiences which an individual may have had can indicate which treatment is likely to succeed and which to fail.

The Treatment of Substance Abuse

Substance abusers nearly always have significant emotional problems and sometimes may have full-blown mental illnesses which call for medication or hospital treatment. Depression, for example, is quite common among drug and alcohol abusers. For this reason, the treatment of the substance abuser should begin with an overall evaluation at a Community Mental Health Center, a psychiatry clinic, or the office of a psychiatrist. In these settings, the appropriate treatment will be recommended, and further specific referrals will be made if necessary.

For those who are frequent heavy users of alcohol or drugs, the first phase of treatment may have to take place in a hospital. This may be necessary because the cessation (the ''withdrawal'') of the drug or alcohol use must be done very carefully, under medical supervision, in order to avoid serious physical complications. Hospital inpatient units for drug and alcohol treatment usually have a full program of therapeutic activities, including individual counseling, group therapy, and family sessions. The hospital stay—usually between two and six weeks—affords an opportunity for a complete assessment of the personal and family problems involved, and a determination of the most appropriate outpatient program to be followed after discharge.

The treatment of drug and alcohol abuse is a long-term undertaking, involving various forms of psychotherapy and counseling. There is no medication which can cure a substance abuser. Treatment, which is done primarily through therapeutic interaction with trained professionals, must go on for many months, or even years. Vocational training, employment counseling, and social service assistance are also important parts of the treatment effort.

Two instances in which medication is used are: (1) some alcoholics are given a drug known as Antabuse, which produces very unpleasant physical effects if the individual drinks alcohol; and (2) in some institutions, heroin addiction is treated by substituting Methadone for heroin. The Methadone itself is a narcotic—although somewhat less harmful than heroin—and must be continued indefinitely. In both these cases, however, the medication is not "curing" the addiction, only masking it or chemically controlling it.

Long-standing patterns of behavior are very difficult to change, and periods of abstinence may be followed by reappearance of the substance abuse behavior. Such relapses are to be expected and can be overcome if the treatment is maintained. Above all else, the substance abuser should be encouraged to continue the treatment program regardless of relapses, setbacks, or apparent failures. Full success may take months or years to achieve, and some treatment programs, for example, Alcoholics Anonymous, must even be continued for life.

Nearly every program for the treatment of substance abusers includes some form of group membership and group support. This may take the form of structured group therapy, more informal group meetings, or unstructured "rap groups" and support networks. The group approach has had considerable success, for several reasons. First of all, abusers tend to trust one another more readily than they trust "outsiders" and will often speak frankly only to one another. In the group setting, no one can be judgmental or superior, since all suffer from the same disease. Secondly, the group offers more availability and support than any one individual can, and the substance abuser's need for support is often very great. In some programs, for example, different group members are available "on call" around the clock to deal with emotional crises in the lives of the other members. Finally, the group functions as a small society, in which the abuser can be rewarded with increasing status as he or she gains increasing mastery over the illness. In lifelong groups, such as Alcoholics Anonymous[5], "recovered" substance abusers become honored leaders and permanent examples to all who follow after them.

References for Further Reading

Chafetz, M., "Alcoholism and Alcoholic Psychoses," in *Comprehensive Textbook of Psychiatry*, edited by Alfred Freedman and Harold Kaplan, 2nd. ed., pp. 1331-1348. Baltimore: The Williams and Wilkins Company, 1975.

Freeman, A., "Opiate Dependence," in *Comprehensive Textbook of Psychiatry*, edited by Alfred Freedman and Harold Kaplan, 2nd. ed., pp. 1298-1317. Baltimore: The Williams and Wilkins Company, 1975.

Grinspoon, L., "Drug Dependence: Nonnarcotic Agents," in *Comprehensive Textbook of Psychiatry*, edited by Alfred Freedman and Harold Kaplan, 2nd. ed., pp. 1317-1330. Baltimore: The Williams and Wilkins Company, 1975.

Goodwin, Donald W., "Alcoholism and Heredity," *Archives of General Psychiatry*, vol. 36 (January, 1979), pp. 57-61.

Manual on Alcoholism. Chicago: American Medical Association, 1977.

 SEVEN

The Person with Brain Disease

Among the many people who consult a clergyperson for emotional problems, it is possible that a few may in reality have serious brain disease, which could be disabling or fatal if not treated. These individuals need the prompt attention of a physician and may need to be hospitalized. The clergyperson may see no more than a half-dozen such cases in an entire career, but in those few instances correct action may mean the difference between life and death. The purpose of this chapter is to help the clergyperson recognize these individuals so that a rapid intervention can be made.

It may seem unlikely at first consideration that a person with serious brain disease would consult a clergyperson rather than a physician, but it does, in fact, occur. The reason for this is that many brain diseases, in addition to causing physical symptoms, have emotional manifestations. These illnesses can cause depression, irritability, changes in personality, or unusual behavior, and it sometimes happens that these are the most evident symptoms. In such a case, the ill person or the family may assume that he or she is simply having an emotional problem, which is appropriate for the clergyperson's attention.

The Organic Brain Syndrome

The group of brain diseases being considered here include such conditions as tumors, diseases of the blood vessels of the brain, conditions
due to normal aging, diseases resulting from injury, drug intoxications,
and many more. Fortunately for our purposes, it is not necessary that
the clergyperson know the specific details of each illness since all of
these various brain diseases result in the same set of characteristic
symptoms. It is as though the brain has only certain ways of reacting
when it is diseased, regardless of the specific nature of that disease.
This characteristic triad of symptoms—known as the Organic Brain
Syndrome—consists of *disorientation, loss of recent memory,* and *impaired level of consciousness.* These three symptoms, either singly or
in combination, are diagnostic of serious brain disease, regardless of
any other emotional disturbances that may be present.

Disorientation

Disorientation refers to the inability to identify correctly time,
place, and person. The individual who is disoriented may not know the
day, the month, or sometimes even the year. The person may not be
able to identify the surroundings or give the name of the community
or city. He or she may not be able to identify other individuals, even
family members or close friends. The disoriented person often makes
guesses to cover up the underlying confusion and may even seem quite
nonchalant about it.

Various degrees of disorientation may occur, from *partial* (for
example, disoriented only to time) to *total* (disoriented to time, place,
and person). Even a partial disorientation is quite significant and should
alert the clergyperson to the possibility of brain disease.

In many cases, it is possible to detect disorientation in the course
of a routine conversation as the individual describes events and daily
activities. In other instances, it is not immediately obvious but becomes
apparent when specific questions are asked about dates, places, and
persons. Evidence for disorientation can also be gathered from the
accounts of those who accompany the individual. The family or friends
may report that the person becomes confused at home, loses track of
dates, or wanders away from the house and cannot get back.

Disorientation often becomes more severe at night when the visual
landmarks of time and place are not available. The family of an ill

person may relate that he or she seems to do well during daylight hours, but becomes confused and agitated at night. This is particularly common among the elderly who suffer from brain impairment due to aging, but it can occur in many other brain diseases as well.

Loss of Recent Memory

The individual with brain disease often shows a characteristic type of memory loss in which recent events cannot be recalled. The person with such a deficit will be able to remember quite well events that occurred months or years before, but will forget the happenings of the previous hours or minutes. In the most severe cases of such a deficit, the individual may lay down an object and be unable to find it after several minutes, or may get up from the dinner table and ask ten minutes later when dinner will be served. Less severe cases are not as obvious, and the ill person may attempt to compensate for memory deficits when questioned by filling in fictitious information in place of the forgotten details.

This phenomenon of impaired recent memory, along with intact memory for remote events, is quite striking and paradoxical. It results from the fact that these two memory functions are carried out by two different areas of the brain, one of which is more susceptible to impairment by disease than the other. Remote memory is so resistant that it remains even when almost all other intellectual functions have ceased.

Like disorientation, memory loss can often be detected during the course of a conversation, or surmised from the accounts of friends or relatives of the ill person. Some simple tests can be used when the situation is unclear or to confirm the presence of a suspected memory deficit. The individual can be told a specific piece of information and then be asked to recall it five or ten minutes later. As an additional test, the person can be shown a simple object, such as a pencil or a set of keys, and then be asked to watch while the object is placed somewhere out of view. After ten minutes of conversation, the person is asked to recall the object and indicate where it is hidden. Individuals who are unable to do these simple tasks should be suspected of having a significant memory deficit.

Impaired Level of Consciousness

Many brain diseases interfere with the individual's ability to remain awake and alert. As the disease progresses, this impairment usually becomes greater and greater. Table 1 presents the technical names and descriptions of the different levels of consciousness, in descending order.

Table 1

Levels of Consciousness

1. "alert"—fully awake and paying attention to all stimuli
2. "drowsy"—awake while participating in conversation, but dozes off when conversation stops
3. "lethargic"—dozes off even while participating in conversation, but can be easily aroused
4. "stuporous"—constantly asleep; can be aroused only with difficulty
5. "comatose"—cannot be aroused

The "alert" person is fully awake and pays attention to what is happening; this is the normal level of consciousness. The "drowsy" individual can pay attention when spoken to directly, but dozes off when the immediate stimulus is taken away. A "lethargic" person is one who dozes off even while spoken to, but can still be aroused easily. With even further impairment, an individual becomes "stuporous" and is difficult to arouse. Finally, the "comatose" person cannot be aroused at all, even with painful stimuli.

Any person who is having difficulty staying awake—except where the cause is simple lack of sleep or boredom—should be considered medically ill until proven otherwise. The lower the level of consciousness, the greater the need for rapid medical intervention. A particularly critical situation is the one in which an individual's level of consciousness is decreasing rapidly, over the course of several hours. This occurs most often after head injuries, but it can be a sign of other conditions as well. Rapidly decreasing level of consciousness is a medical emergency of the first order, and the individual with this symptom should be taken to the emergency room of the nearest hospital without delay.

Dealing with the Brain-Diseased Individual

A person showing any or all of the symptoms of the Organic Brain Syndrome should have a medical evaluation as soon as possible. The clergyperson may find, however, that a medical referral is met with considerable resistance, either on the part of the ill person or the family.

The proper understanding and handling of this resistance is particularly important, since some of these illnesses may be fatal if not attended to right away.

Resistance from the Ill Person

Brain disease is among the most disabling of all medical conditions because it destroys the individual's ability to perceive reality and exercise judgment. In this sense it is even more devastating than a total physical paralysis. The brain-diseased person is likely to be confused and frightened, unable to think clearly or understand what is happening. In these individuals, a vicious cycle frequently takes place, in which disorientation and memory loss lead to mounting anxiety, which in turn impairs orientation and memory even further. The overall result is a spiral of increasing confusion and agitation.

In dealing with a brain-diseased individual, therefore, the clergyperson must take special measures to decrease the ill person's anxiety and confusion. The interview should be held in a quiet room in which the lighting is adequate but not overly bright. A comfortable chair should be provided, if possible. The clergyperson's general manner should be calm and unhurried, yet to the point. He or she should speak slowly, keeping sentences brief and grammatically simple. The ill person should be given only as much information as is necessary to obtain cooperation; all extraneous information should be eliminated. "Overloading" a brain-diseased person with unnecessary details often causes confusion and increased resistance.

Brain-diseased individuals, if their illness is not too far advanced, are frequently aware of their disability and are intensely distressed at their difficulty in thinking clearly. At the same time, pride and fear may prevent them from acknowledging their condition and accepting treatment. The clergyperson must treat such persons with particular tact and patience if a successful referral is to be made. Honesty is essential, and the individual should be told clearly that he or she may have a serious illness. At the same time, the clergyperson should be sensitive to the ill person's dignity and fears and should not push too quickly for action. As in all medical and psychiatric illnesses, the treatment is likely to be much more successful if it is accepted willingly and cooperatively, rather than submitted to under duress.

The exception to this rule, as already noted, is the case where the individual's level of consciousness is decreasing rapidly. In such a situation, the person must be transported to a hospital right away, regardless of resistance or embarrassment.

Resistance from the Family

To the average layperson, the idea of brain disease is quite frightening. One might think that this fear would motivate family members to get help for the ill person as quickly as possible, but it often has the opposite effect: the family may deny the illness and refuse treatment. A statement sometimes heard from family members in these situations is, "We'll take him home and take care of him there—he doesn't need to go to a hospital." Since some of these illnesses are potentially fatal if not treated, it is very important that the clergyperson break through this resistance.

The same guidelines laid out in chapter 2 should be followed in these situations. The clergyperson must understand the sources of the family's resistance and must beware of his or her own resistance as well. This situation is especially difficult to handle because the family's worst fears may be borne out: the individual may indeed have a fatal illness. The clergyperson should therefore not try to minimize the fear or cover it over with excessive reassurance. It can be stated honestly, however, that many brain diseases *are* completely curable, even those which cause very marked symptoms. If the ill person is young, and if the symptoms have appeared rather suddenly within the previous two or three weeks, the chances of the condition being curable are fairly good. The following case is an example of such an illness.

Mr. Y, a thirty-seven-year-old married attorney, began to experience frequent headaches and became irritable and somewhat depressed. Since he had had emotional problems in the past, he and his wife both assumed that these new symptoms were also due to emotional causes. He talked with his pastor and was thinking about making an appointment at a local counseling center. He had undergone a physical examination three months earlier which was completely normal.

About ten days after the onset of the headaches, Mrs. Y noticed that her husband seemed somewhat forgetful and confused. One day he had some trouble finding his way home from the office.

That same night, Mrs. Y awoke at 2 A.M. to find Mr. Y wandering through the house, mumbling in a confused manner.

At this point, Mrs. Y brought her husband to the emergency room of a nearby general hospital, where he was examined and admitted immediately to the neurology service. Tests revealed that Mr. Y had a brain infection which required surgery and antibiotic treatment. These procedures were done, and he recovered without complication. He left the hospital after three weeks and returned to his usual routines, completely cured.

Senile Dementia

The most common brain disease which the clergyperson is likely to encounter among his or her parishioners is Senile Dementia, the condition of brain deterioration which sometimes accompanies old age. The number of persons in our society over the age of sixty-five has increased markedly in the past half-century as medical science has found new ways to prolong life and control disease. The average clergyperson may now find that a large proportion of his or her time is spent in ministering to elderly members of the congregation or in counseling their families who are caring for them.

A complete discussion of Senile Dementia and all of its associated problems is beyond the scope of this book, but several points should be made here about the illness. (Several useful books and articles on this subject are cited in the references at the end of this chapter.) It usually begins during the late sixties or seventies and is characterized by the presence of the Organic Brain Syndrome. There is a state of slowly increasing disorientation and confusion, with defects in recent memory and periods of drowsiness. In advanced cases, there may be hallucinations and delusional thinking as well.

It must be stated, however, that this disease is not an inevitable consequence of aging. Many older people function well into their seventies and eighties without any significant brain impairment. The actual incidence of senile brain disease among people over sixty-five is thought to be 10-20 percent.[1]

When the disease does develop, there is no cause for either the ill person or the family to feel guilty or regretful, as though it could have been "avoided" by any kind of precautions in the past. As far as we know at this time, there is no specific way that Senile Dementia can be avoided if the individual has the genetic predisposition for the illness. Unfortunately, it is not even possible to identify those people who have this genetic predisposition.

The disease is believed to be the end result of a gradual loss of brain cells. This slow loss of cells actually occurs in every person throughout life, because the brain is not capable of regenerating new cells to replace old ones which cease to function. Since we are born with many millions of brain cells, this slow loss does not have any effect until an advanced age is attained. Even then, it is not clear why some persons develop Senile Dementia while others do not.

Physicians have been searching for a medical treatment for Senile Dementia for many years. A number of methods have been tried, but none has really been successful. In recent years, articles have appeared in lay magazines reporting on new "wonder drugs" which can reverse the aging process of the brain, but these findings have not as yet been substantiated by medical research. Given these facts, the clergyperson is advised at this time not to hold out any great hopes for successful medical treatment of an individual with Senile Dementia. Instead, it is much more fruitful to focus on minimizing the individual's discomfort and maximizing those strengths and abilities which remain intact. If this can be done, many of these people can be cared for within their own homes and families.

Occasionally, an illness which appears at first to be Senile Dementia proves later to be depression, a condition which *is* treatable. Because of this possibility—albeit a slim one—every individual with symptoms of Senile Dementia should have a psychiatric evaluation.

Anxiety and confusion are key factors in the functioning of an individual with Senile Dementia. When anxiety is low, the elderly person can often do quite well, within a limited range of activity. He or she may be able to care for basic physical needs, maintain hygiene, participate in social activities, and show good intellectual capabilities. When anxiety and confusion interfere, however, all of these capabilities deteriorate rapidly, and bewildered agitation can result. The effective management of a person with Senile Dementia, then, becomes largely a matter of keeping anxiety and confusion at a minimum.

The comments which follow are phrased in terms of the individual with Senile Dementia who is cared for at home, within an extended family. This does not imply that all such individuals can—or should—

be kept at home. The decision must be made based on the circumstances and feelings of each elderly individual and each family. These management considerations, however, apply equally well to elderly persons in retirement homes and geriatric facilities.

One of the main ways to avoid anxiety and confusion in a person with Senile Dementia is to make sure that the individual is well oriented to time and place. Large, easy-to-read clocks and calendars should be readily available. Lighting should always be adequate, and a small light should be left on during the night in or near the bedroom. Confusion in maneuvering around the house can be avoided by marking the doors of the rooms with small signs or symbols. Outdoor exercise should be encouraged, but care should be taken that the individual not become lost and unable to find the way home. Written instructions or a simple map can be useful in this regard.

Repetitive daily routines become very important to the individual with Senile Dementia and serve as an anchor in reality. When he or she knows that certain activities always take place on certain days, this helps greatly in maintaining orientation to time. The family should be encouraged to set up some simple household routines for each day of the week in which the elderly person can participate. The nature of the routines is not as important as the fact that they occur predictably, on the same day, week after week.

If routines must be changed, the elderly person should be told of the change well in advance, and time should be allowed for explanation and questions. It is always advisable to tell the person about changes beforehand, even if the news causes some emotional upset. It is far more damaging to expose an elderly person to a sudden, unexpected disruption of routines.

The family of a person with Senile Dementia should be helped to accept the fact that all their dealings with that person must be carried out slowly, carefully, and with a good deal of patience. The individual's disabilities should always be taken into account, but at the same time the family should avoid treating the elderly person as totally helpless. Strengths and capabilities which are still intact should be used as much as possible, for too much passivity and dependence can be very destructive to the individual's emotional state. Success in caring for such a person depends on the family's ability to tread the fine line between the two extremes of expecting too much and expecting too little.

References for Further Reading

Berezin, M. A., in "The Elderly Person," in *The Harvard Guide to Modern Psychiatry,* edited by Armand Nicholi. Cambridge: Harvard University Press, 1978.

Butler, Robert, *Why Survive? Being Old in America.* New York: Harper & Row, Publishers, Inc., 1975.

Seltzer, B., and Frazier, S. H., "Organic Mental Disorders," in *The Harvard Guide to Modern Psychiatry,* edited by Armand Nicholi. Cambridge: Harvard University Press, 1978.

Usdin, Gene, ed., *Aging: The Process and the People.* New York: Brunner/Mazel, Inc., 1978.

Weinberg, J., "Geriatric Psychiatry," in *Comprehensive Textbook of Psychiatry,* edited by Alfred Freedman and Harold Kaplan, 2nd. ed. Baltimore: The Williams and Wilkins Company, 1975.

Weinberg, Jack, "What Do I Say to My Mother When I Have Nothing to Say?" *Geriatrics* (November, 1974), pp. 155-159.

 EIGHT

Psychological Factors in Physical Illness

Ministering to the needs of the physically ill has been a vital part of the clergy's role for centuries and continues to be so. The clergyperson's support and comfort and the emotional power of religious rituals are as important to the ill person today as ever before—perhaps even more important in this age of confusing and often impersonal medical technology. As medical science's understanding of health and illness has increased over the past half-century, the importance of emotional and psychological factors has become more and more apparent. This chapter will review some of the recent findings of psychosomatic research. The implication of these findings is that, in addition to providing reassurance and comfort, the clergyperson's interventions may actually help to bring about a significant change in the disease process.

Psychosomatics

"Psychosomatics" is the area of medical research which tries to understand the relationship between psychological factors and physical illness. The name itself is formed from the union of two Greek words, *psyche* and *soma*. *Soma* means "body" and refers to the physical

113

structure of the human body with all of its biochemical and physiological mechanisms. The word *psyche* is more difficult to translate but is usually taken to mean either "mind" or "soul"; it refers to the entire psychological aspect of the human being, including thoughts, feelings, beliefs, memories, emotional conflicts, and aspirations. Psychosomatics, then, is the study of the interrelationship of *psyche* and *soma*, as manifested in physical illnesses.

One may ask why the focus of psychosomatics is on diseases, rather than on the interrelationship of *psyche* and *soma* in states of health. The interrelationship in normal functioning seems to be so enormously complex that it would be almost impossible to decipher each step and describe the overall process. When, however, one aspect of physical functioning breaks down and a disease develops, that one part of the overall system becomes more obvious by its malfunctioning and is therefore easier to study. It has often happened in medicine that the study of a disease has led to a greater understanding of healthy physiology. In the same way, it is hoped that by studying the workings of *soma* and *psyche* in disease, we will ultimately reach an understanding of how they interact in the state of health.

History of Psychosomatic Theory

A brief review of disease concepts at various stages of history will help to put modern psychosomatic theory in perspective.

In prehistoric times, as far as can be determined, people believed that disease was caused by invading spirits and unseen supernatural entities. These forces, it was believed, took hold of a person because of sins or errors which had been committed, or sometimes for inexplicable reasons. Disease was seen as a punishment and a form of divine retribution, and its prevention and cure could only be achieved by placating the supernatural beings. Primitive people apparently had a holistic concept of illness, with no dichotomy between afflictions of the mind and those of the body.

The Egyptians and Babylonians, while developing some new treatment techniques, adhered by and large to the concept of disease as divine retribution. The later Assyrians (about 500 B.C.) were evidently the first to think of disease as being the result of something going wrong within the individual, rather than strictly the result of an outside invader. This was an important innovation, but the Assyrians still retained the idea of divine punishment and advised sacrifices to the spirits as therapy for illness.

The Greeks took over from the Assyrians the idea of disease originating within the body and developed the concept to a higher degree of sophistication. Between the years 400 and 100 B.C., the Greeks, led by the great physician Hippocrates, developed an intricate theory in which disease was the result of imbalances of various fluids in the body. The Greek physicians were keen observers and classifiers of diseases, and they described very effectively many of the illnesses which we still encounter today. They recognized that the emotions could affect the body and that fear, anger, and depression could bring about illness.

The roles of physician and priest in ancient Greece were closely related. Healing ceremonies took place in temple settings where the individual's emotional and spiritual state was attended to as much as his or her body. *Psyche* and *soma* were indivisible.

This way of thinking extended after the Greeks into the Roman period, in which the tradition of scientific observation was carried still further. The Roman physicians continued the classification of illnesses and the holistic approach which was laid down by their predecessors.

With the decline of the Roman Empire, Europe entered the Middle Ages, and the theory of disease underwent a major transformation. During the thousand years between 500 and 1500 A.D., the objective scientific tradition of the Greeks and Romans was neglected and soon forgotten, and there was a return of the belief in spirits, demons, witches, and divine retribution. Medicine in the Middle Ages was dominated once again by magical thinking and a supernatural orientation. But at the same time, the physicians of the Middle Ages continued to recognize the interrelationship of the spirit and the body, and the importance of faith in bringing about physical healing.

In the Renaissance period, between 1500 and 1750, there was a renewal of interest in the Greco-Roman scientific tradition of medicine. The Renaissance marks the beginning of modern science and the re-awakening of interest in the rational, scientific observation and study of the physical world. At the same time, however, a significant conceptual problem developed, one which was to plague medicine for the next three hundred years. This problem was the split between the mind and the body. *Psyche* and *soma* came to be regarded for the first time in history as two separate entities, and it was believed that while the *soma* was worthy of scientific study, the *psyche* was not. The *psyche* was ignored more and more by medical science as the idea of the significant influence of the emotions on the body was rejected.

This trend continued through the eighteenth century and into the nineteenth. Great advances were made in the understanding of disease, but the *psyche* remained ignored and the mind-body split grew wider than ever.

In the later years of the nineteenth century, however, a small group of physicians began to pay more attention to the effects of psychological states on physical illness. One of these men was the French neurologist Jean Martin Charcot, who was able to demonstrate that changes in physical symptoms could be produced through hypnosis. Among Charcot's pupils in 1885 was a young physician named Sigmund Freud, who was later to be responsible in large measure for bringing *psyche* and *soma* together again in medical thinking.

Freud began his career as a general physician and neurologist, and he retained an interest in physical diseases throughout his life. As early as 1895, when he published his *Studies on Hysteria,*[1] he was convinced that emotional factors played a key role in the genesis and course of physical illness. His ideas were met with disbelief and criticism; Victorian Viennese society was not yet ready to take its private emotions out of hiding. When Freud continued his teaching and his research into his patients' intimate feelings, his critics grew more vociferous and he was officially censured by the Vienna Medical Society. But his ideas began to take hold, and he lived to see them accepted and acclaimed in Europe and America. While many of Freud's specific theories have not stood the test of time, his basic premise concerning the role of emotions in physical illness has been resoundingly confirmed by fifty years of research and observation.

In the United States, Dr. Franz Alexander was one of those who carried on Freud's psychosomatic theories and brought them into line with the findings of later research. Alexander, a psychiatrist and product of the Viennese school of psychoanalysis, came to this country in 1930 and took a position at the University of Chicago. He and his colleagues devoted a major effort over the next twenty years to the intense psychoanalytic study of patients with a variety of chronic physical illnesses. Their findings were published in the form of two books[2] which are classics of psychosomatics research. The following two cases are illustrative of Alexander's clinical data and his analysis of that data:

> Mrs. S. G., aged 28 years, developed painful, stiff muscles immediately after she discovered that her husband had had a love affair. After persistent pain and stiffness of the muscles for a few months, she developed arthritis. Her mother was a conscientious but cold woman; the father had deserted the family when the patient was two years old. She was very competitive with an older brother and spent much of her childhood in outdoor activities. She felt that her mother's role, and the position of women in general, was unbearable and said openly she would rather die than tell her husband she loved him, even if she did. "Then I could never be on top." She refused sexual intercourse for several months after marriage, had never had an orgasm, and agreed only infrequently to sexual relations. Although her husband had been a prize fighter and she was a frail-appearing little woman, she always headed the household and made the decisions, directing her three young daughters in assisting her excellent housekeeping. Her husband's infidelity was the first indication of his rebellion and of her inability to compete with him and control him. When frustrated in her competition the hostility increased, found no outlet, and the muscle soreness and arthritis followed.[3]

The second case, that of a man with hyperthyroid disease, is an example of the premature need for self-sufficiency which Alexander found in many of these patients.

> H. D., a 35-year-old single man, the last of eight children, is the only surviving male. Two older brothers died at age 10 and 3 respectively, and one brother died at home one week after birth when the patient was two. His father was a puritanical man who was harsh and impersonal to hide his own weakness and insecurity. He was apparently demonstrative of affection and fondled his children as long as they were helpless infants but demanded adult behavior as soon as they were able to walk and talk. The mother was depreciated by the father because she had had an illegitimate child in her adolescence . . . and was married "out of pity" by the patient's father. She was unable to stand up to the father and

during the patient's infancy worked in the family store for several years. The father prevented the mother as well as the older sisters from giving the patient much attention. After the patient entered the first grade, his father insisted that no one read him the funny papers any more because he should learn to read for himself. Constant pressure was brought to bear on him to behave like an adult and yet he was continually restricted in the active pursuit of his interests.[4]

Alexander was able to demonstrate that each of his patients had significant conflicts regarding the expression of certain emotions. When stressful life events stirred up these conflicts, flare-ups of the disease would result. Alexander believed that each disease was linked with a specific emotional conflict; for example, ulcer patients had conflicts over dependency, while hypertensives had inner conflicts about the expression of anger. This idea came to be known as the "specificity theory" of psychosomatics.

Alexander's work provided many insights into the relation of *psyche* and *soma,* but the specificity aspect of his theory was not borne out by later studies. The neat one-to-one correspondence of specific emotional conflicts and specific diseases began to break down as more and more cases were investigated. The role of genetic predisposition, personality, and individual coping style has become increasingly evident with continued research. It now seems clear that many different environmental stresses and emotional conflicts can precipitate illness in individuals who are genetically predisposed to particular diseases.

Present-Day Psychosomatic Theory

In the present state of psychosomatic knowledge, we do not yet have one unifying theory to apply to all diseases. What we have instead is a growing number of fascinating pieces of a puzzle, some of which fit together, while others do not. Our understanding of the causation of illness can be summed up by Figure 1. Illness is thought of as being the end result of the interaction of four different factors.

Genetic predisposition makes an individual more susceptible to one illness than to another and explains why certain diseases seem to run in families. Scientists are not yet able to observe specific genes or predict a specific individual's susceptibilities, but we feel certain that these predispositions exist. *Toxic and infectious agents* are obviously

Figure 1

The Components of Disease Causation

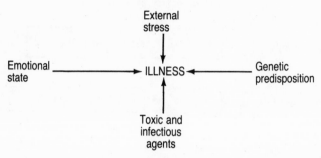

important as well. Tuberculosis cannot develop unless certain bacteria are present, and lead poisoning is clearly the result of a toxic agent in the environment. Similarly, some forms of cancer may one day prove to be transmitted by viruses. The effect of *stressful life events* in precipitating diseases seems to be considerable. Some studies have shown a high correlation between disease onset and the presence of such stressful events as divorce, bereavement, injury, or loss of work. Even such seemingly positive events as marriage or the birth of a child can be quite stressful, and illness can sometimes develop after these life events. Finally, the *emotional state* of the individual, aside from major external stresses, is an important determinant of health and disease. The observation made by Hippocrates and Aristotle over two thousand years ago has been confirmed by modern research: intense feeling-states, such as anger, depression, and hopelessness, do seem to play a role in both bringing about and prolonging physical illness.

The relationship of emotions and disease is actually two-sided. A state of emotional distress, as we have said, can contribute to the onset of disease. Once the disease is established, however, it can also *create* further emotional difficulties, both in the patient and in his or her family. What finally results in many cases is a vicious cycle of mounting emotional distress and worsening illness. (This process is summarized in Figure 2.) The cycle can be broken by medical treatment of the disease process or by therapeutic human interaction aimed at changing the feeling-state. The ideal treatment should include both of these approaches.

Figure 2

Interrelationships of Emotional
Distress and Disease

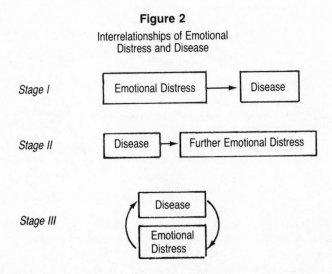

The latter point needs some emphasizing. In recent years there has been a great deal of interest in spiritual healing and "holistic medicine." As we have seen earlier in this chapter, the holistic concept is by no means new but is as important today as in the days of the ancient Greeks. Truly holistic healing, however, requires that the clergyperson, the mental health professional, and the medical physician work *together*, and not in place of each other. In any case where a physical illness exists, psychological or spiritual methods should never be the sole treatment modality.

The following sections of this chapter will deal with psychosomatic theory in regard to two specific areas, infectious diseases and cancer. These two areas are chosen as representative of the many exciting research developments occurring in the larger field. Covering the entire field is beyond the scope of this chapter, but the references at the end will point the way for the interested reader.

Infectious Diseases

In the late nineteenth century, a major breakthrough in medical research occurred with the discovery of bacteria. For the first time, it became possible to isolate and observe directly the causative agent of a disease and to design a treatment specifically for that disease. In the wave of enthusiasm which followed the discovery of microorganisms, many scientists felt that the answer to all human suffering had been found. It would be only a matter of time, they believed, before all germs would be isolated and identified and all illnesses cured.

Within fifteen or twenty years after the discovery of microorganisms, however, some puzzling questions began to present themselves. The "germ" theory predicted that everyone who was exposed to bacteria would develop disease, but in fact this was not true. If 100 people, for example, were exposed to the same bacteria, they did not all become ill. While 65 or 70 would be affected, there might be 30 or 35 who did not become ill at all. Furthermore, among the 65 or 70 who did develop disease, many different degrees of sickness would be observed. Some individuals might become severely ill and die; others would recover in a matter of weeks; and still others might have a very mild illness and recover within days. It was clear that another factor was operating. The presence of bacteria did not explain everything.

After many years of research, scientists were finally able to isolate what we now know as the "immune system" of the human body. This is the body's defense system which is responsible for fighting off and destroying any invading foreign particles or organisms. It is the functioning of this system which determines in large part whether or not an individual becomes ill after being exposed to germs and also determines the severity of that illness.

The front-line "soldiers" of the immune system are the so-called "white blood cells." These very specialized cells have the capacity to recognize any particle which is not part of the body and to destroy or inactivate that particle. These white cells, however, do not act independently; they seem to be under the control of a long "chain of command" which regulates their functioning. Figure 3 presents a schematic diagram of this system of nerves and hormones which regulates the activity of the immune system.

White blood cells are sensitive to the effects of a hormone, cortisol, which is secreted by the adrenal gland. When the level of circulating cortisol goes up, the white cells seem to become less effective. The adrenal gland, which produces the cortisol, is itself under the control of another hormone, which is known by its abbreviated name, ACTH. This substance is secreted by the pituitary gland, which lies at the base of the brain. Finally, the pituitary gland is connected by many nerve pathways to the higher parts of the brain, areas which are involved with the whole range of an individual's thoughts, feelings, beliefs, memories, and aspirations. In other words, we have reason to believe that the white blood cells are at the end of a long pathway of control which begins in the highest levels of the brain. Through this pathway, it is possible that the individual's emotional state can exert a constant influence over the body's ability to fight infection.[5]

In this interaction of emotions and the immune system, depression seems to play a key role. It has been demonstrated that during some forms of depression, there is an increase in the blood level of cortisol and a corresponding decrease in the effectiveness of the white blood

Figure 3

The Chain of Command of the
Immune System

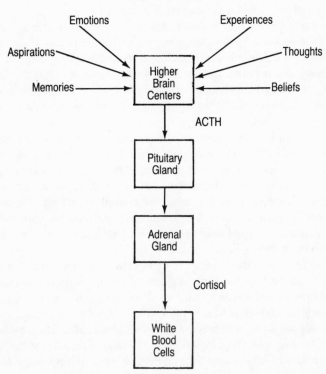

cells. These findings would lead one to predict that depressed individuals will be more susceptible to infectious diseases or will have a harder time fighting off these diseases. A recent study was done to test this very hypothesis.

The study was done on a military installation, at a time when an influenza epidemic was occurring in the surrounding area and was expected to spread to the base. All the soldiers on the base were given a psychological test which was designed to measure depression. When the outbreak of influenza occurred, most of the servicemen became ill, but it was observed that they fell into two groups: those who recovered in an average of one week, and those who needed three weeks or more to return to health. The significant finding was that the slow recoverers had all shown significantly more depression on the psychological test than the rapid recoverers.[6]

Another interesting piece of research had to do with the healing of wounds, another process in which the immune system plays a very important part. In order to recover from any type of wound, be it traumatic or surgical, one must have a well-functioning immune system. In this study, the subjects were patients who were recovering from surgery for detached retina. This illness was selected because the healing retina can be observed directly and the rate of healing can be plotted very precisely. The patients were interviewed before the surgery and were rated on certain items which reflected depression. They were also asked about their expectations regarding the outcome of the surgery, about the confidence they felt in their surgeon, and about their confidence in their own ability to cope, regardless of the outcome.

The quality of the surgery in each case was equal, and all the patients received the same post-operative care. Each patient's rate of healing was monitored, and the rates were compared. It was found that the patients who healed most quickly and had the fewest complications were those who had faith in the future, who were optimistic, and who felt confident that they would be able to carry on no matter how the surgery turned out. The authors concluded the study by saying:

> . . . rapid healing occur[s] . . . when the patient has faith in the healer, his methods of healing, and feels that those methods are relevant to the cause of illness. . . . the person seeking to help the slow healer should . . . focus primarily on what variables enhance or destroy the patient's attitude of expectant faith.[7]

Cancer

It is no exaggeration to say that cancer is the most dreaded of all physical illnesses. While it is not the leading cause of death in this country—heart disease still ranks higher—cancer exacts a huge toll of human suffering, both from its victims and from their families. For the past four decades, this grim killer has been studied intensively from every point of view, and psychosomatics has made some important contributions to this endeavor.

It has long been known that in many forms of cancer, the disease can have a prolonged course, in which acute flare-ups alternate with extended periods of remission. In most instances, the reasons for the acute flare-ups are not at all clear, and on the surface it often appears that there is no predictable pattern to the illness. But physicians who have worked closely with cancer patients have suspected that emotional factors have a great deal to do with the course of the illness. Cancer patients with confidence and a strong sense of determination sometimes surprise their doctors by living much longer than expected. On the other hand, patients who seem to lose their "will to live" and become despondent often deteriorate and die, in spite of the best medical care.

In the late 1940s psychiatrist Dr. William Greene, of the University of Rochester, began an intensive study of a small group of patients with cancers of the blood and lymph nodes. This particular form of cancer was chosen because it typically has a long course, with many remissions and exacerbations. Dr. Greene's hypothesis was that the ups and downs of each patient's illness would correlate with changes in that patient's emotional state and with the stressful events of his or her life.

Over a period of four years, Dr. Greene and his associates kept close track of each patient's major life events, physical status, and emotional condition. They also reviewed each patient's past history in detail. The results of the study, published in 1954 and 1956, were striking: there was indeed a close relationship between flare-ups of the cancer process and life stresses, particularly depressions which followed separations from loved ones through death, divorce, or leaving home.[8] Two of Dr. Greene's cases are here summarized.

A 35-year-old man, an only child, was apparently very aggressive, worked consistently, and made progressive advancement in his work. His history indicated he was basically dependent, and had a very ambivalent relation with both of his parents. He had had the unusual experience of living with his mother until the age of 5, when the father rejoined the family group. Two years after the birth of his daughter, and a year after the birth of his son, his father died suddenly. . . . He then had moderate grief reaction, and 6 months later [swelling of the lymph nodes] was first recognized. Biopsy showed Hodgkin's disease.[9]

A 37-year-old man had always had a close relationship with his mother and a distant relationship with his father. After the war he returned to his home, his first experience there since his mother's death, which occurred while he was in the service. He invested all his savings in a theatrical venture which failed. At the same time he found out that his girl friend was already married. He became increasingly depressed, weeping without apparent provocation, and talking of how worthless and unsuccessful he was. After a year of these symptoms, an enlarged cervical node was first recognized, and . . . on biopsy showed Hodgkin's disease.[10]

One of the most fascinating aspects of the Greene study was that the researchers were able in a few cases to predict when future exacerbations of the illness would occur. The following case is one in which the prediction was borne out by the illness.

This patient had chronic myelocytic leukemia. It was predicted that if and when her only son, the youngest child, got married, she would probably have a relapse. At the time of this prediction she was in a clinical remission induced by administration of [drugs]. She was then symptomatically well, pursued her usual energetic activity as a teacher, and helped with arrangements for the marriage of her youngest daughter. Five months later her son became engaged. At this time the patient developed progressive cough, fever, and sadness and was admitted to the hospital 2 weeks later with a severe exacerbation which subsided after use of radiation therapy. Three months later her son's engagement was publicly announced and a week later she was admitted to the hospital again in relapse. Three months thereafter the son was married, but the patient was too sick to attend the wedding and had to be admitted to the hospital 2 days afterward. No therapy was effective and she died 3 weeks later.[11]

The Greene study was one of the pioneering efforts in this branch of cancer research. But like many pioneers, the author was ahead of his time, and it took nearly twenty years for other researchers to discover a physiologic mechanism to explain his findings. In the interim, a considerable number of other studies confirmed Dr. Greene's hypothesis and added more evidence of the important role of emotions in cancer.[12]

Some basic facts about the physiology of cancer will help the reader to understand the theories which follow. Cancer begins to develop when a single cell, in some organ of the body, becomes abnormal and begins to multiply rapidly. The abnormal cells soon start to damage the surrounding normal tissue and to use up large amounts of nutrients. The body starves while the cancer grows. In time, the cancer cells spread to other parts of the body and seriously impair the functioning of vital organs.

The key question in understanding cancer is: What causes the original cell to become abnormal? In the past, it was believed that some external agent—radiation, a chemical poison, a bacterium, or a virus—attacked the cell and caused the malignant change to occur. Research efforts have been aimed at isolating these causative agents, and in a few types of cancer they have at least tentatively been identified. For most cancers, however, this theory has been inadequate.

In more recent years, a different hypothesis has been proposed to explain the genesis of cancer. According to this newer view, abnormal cells are not created by external agents but are produced by the body itself in the course of its normal operation. Most organs of the body are constantly losing old cells and regenerating new ones; like any factory production line, each organ occasionally turns out a defective product. If this is so, however, why do we not all develop cancerous diseases? The answer lies in the immune system, which functions as a kind of "quality control" mechanism. In the healthy individual, it is argued, the white blood cells maintain a constant surveillance over the body and can quickly recognize and destroy any abnormal cells which are produced. Cancer develops—in the genetically predisposed individual—when the immune system fails to carry out this function.

The psychosomatic implications of this "surveillance" theory are immense. As was described above, the immune system is under the control of a long "chain of command" in which emotional factors could play a large part. The suppression of the immune system, particularly in states of prolonged depression, could lead not only to infectious illnesses, but also to the development of cancer. The observations made by Greene nearly thirty years ago become even more impressive in light of this new hypothesis.

Another bit of evidence supporting this theory comes from personality studies of cancer patients. These studies have shown that cancer victims, particularly those who do poorly in treatment, are often people who deny unpleasant feelings and keep their emotions hidden. These individuals frequently have a history of chronic depression, which they struggle to hide and for which they never seek help. One can hypothesize that these patients are genetically predisposed to cancer, and that their immune systems are suppressed for long periods of time, allowing the disease to develop.

Counseling the Physically Ill Individual

Although many specific details remain unclear, the general principle that emotions play an important role in the genesis and course of many physical illnesses could almost be considered an accepted fact. Members of the clergy can have a considerable impact upon the emotional state of those who seek their help and can therefore be instrumental both in preventing disease and in speeding recovery from illness. The following suggestions apply to situations in which the clergyperson is counseling an individual who has a diagnosed medical illness of a chronic nature. It goes without saying that any person with *unexplained* physical symptoms should be urged to see a physician before any counseling is begun.

Recent psychosomatic research has shown that many people with chronic physical illnesses have great difficulty in putting their emotions into words. The astute observer can often see these feelings expressed through nonverbal means—tearing of the eyes, reddening of the face, nervous twitching of the body, etc.—but the patient is often unaware of these emotional phenomena. This characteristic has been called "alexithymia," meaning literally "lack of words for moods."[13]

If the clergyperson is dealing with an individual who has such difficulties, it is advisable not to push the patient to express feelings. The individual will probably speak mostly of the illness and its symptoms, and the clergyperson can encourage such conversation, all the while listening for evidence of underlying feelings. One should be particularly attentive to comments indicating recent losses, environmental stresses, or depression. Familiarity with the many varied symptoms of depression (see chapter 5) will be very useful in this situation.

While listening to the patient's account of the illness, the clergyperson should begin forming hypothetical links between stresses and depressions and the onset or worsening of the illness. Special attention should be paid to the family context in which the physical symptoms occur. Does the ulcer patient have attacks of pain after arguments with his spouse, or does the diabetic child become ill at a time when the parents are threatening each other with separation? These associations will probably not be revealed directly, but they can be uncovered by some skillful questioning. As in the case of many psychiatric illnesses, the symptoms may be manifestations of serious family problems. If this is so, the treatment must include attention to these family issues.

Some clergy are hesitant to deal in any depth with the medically ill because of their lack of detailed understanding of physical illnesses. It should be emphasized that for our purposes, the clergyperson need not know any technical information about medical conditions. Physical symptoms should be thought of in this context as signals which may indicate the presence of emotional problems. The clergyperson's ultimate aim should be to uncover the underlying emotional sickness and to facilitate its healing.

At some point during the interaction with the patient, the clergyperson must make explicit the link between the patient's emotional distress and his or her physical symptoms, if such a link appears to exist. The correct timing of this move is very important; it must be done at a moment when the patient's trust is sufficiently high that he or she will take the concept seriously and not reject it out of hand. In a few cases, this can be done in a first interview; in other cases, the clergyperson may have to wait days or even weeks until the moment is appropriate.

When the link between physical disease and emotions is first proposed, a frequent response on the patient's part is, "So you're saying it's all in my head, right?" This is usually said in a frightened or angry voice and reflects the patient's fear, both of the underlying emotions and of rejection by the clergyperson. When the subject of feelings is brought up, patients often jump to the conclusion that they are about to be sent off to some type of frightening psychiatric treatment or to an "insane asylum." The clergyperson must be prepared to answer this comment in a supportive but honest way.

It is essential, first of all, to acknowledge that the patient's physical pain and disability are completely real, not imagined or feigned. The point should then be made that real illnesses can sometimes be caused, or worsened, by unexpressed emotional feelings which are also *real*, and are usually not esoteric or difficult to understand. It is sometimes useful to use the analogy of the emotions being like steam inside an engine, which, if not released periodically, can build up high pressure and cause damage to the machinery. Finally, the message should be given that the clergyperson will remain available for support and guidance throughout the course of whatever treatment is necessary. If all of this can be said in a warm, nondefensive manner, the way may be opened for therapeutic exploration of feelings.

Nearly all patients with chronic physical illnesses can benefit from counseling, and some should be considered for psychiatric treatment. If significant depression, psychotic symptoms, suicidal thinking, or serious family problems are present, the patient should be urged to have a psychiatric evaluation. The clergyperson can be extremely helpful in setting up such a referral and encouraging the patient to follow it through. If the emotional difficulties seem to be of a lesser magnitude, the clergyperson may be able to do the counseling alone, but it is always advisable that he or she keep in touch with the treating medical physician, and sometimes with a psychiatric consultant as well.

In the ideal treatment setting, the clergyperson and the medical physician would have an open channel of communication between them, and mutual respect for each other's role in the overall plan of therapy. Unfortunately, this ideal is not always attained. Despite the growing mass of psychosomatics research, some physicians do not take seriously the role of the emotional and the spiritual in physical disease. But on the other side of the fence, a similar phenomenon has occurred: some clergy, like other members of our society, have lost faith in medicine as a viable treatment method. It is hoped that open-minded clergy and open-minded physicians will find their way to each other, for their patients and parishioners have much to gain from their cooperation.

A Case Report

The following case report, taken from recent psychosomatic literature, is presented as a conclusion to this chapter. It illustrates the efficacy of psychotherapy in the treatment of a life-threatening physical illness.

Ms. A, a 64-year-old obese mother of nine, had been married for 47 years at the time of consultation. [She had been attending a hypertension clinic for two years and had been treated with a variety of medications.] Despite this intensive treatment, Ms. A had shown no noticeable consistent reduction in blood pressure since she began attending the clinic. She reported that she felt well both physically and mentally. She was considered free of psychiatric difficulty by both her physician and herself, and she had no psychiatric history or previous treatment. The psychological consultation [the author is a psychologist] was performed on the request of the therapist whose interest was piqued by the high blood pressure readings and the inability of the patient to profit from high doses of five powerful antihypertensive agents.

Ms. A appeared to be a nice, quiet, cooperative, affable, neatly dressed woman who looked younger than her stated age. The initial interview consisted of general, open-ended questions regarding her life situation. She did not hesitate to report frustrations [in her marriage]. She stated that her husband was arrogant, insensitive, hypercritical, jealous, and unable to listen to her. She elaborated that his personality had been more bothersome to her recently since her youngest child had left home. She felt that she was now more dependent on her husband than at any previous time in their relationship. Ms. A was also upset by what she felt was an insufficient amount of contact with all of her children. She reported feeling lonely and isolated since her last child left home and wished her children would initiate more contact with her. . . .

Ms. A requested further interviews and was seen individually in once weekly psychotherapy for several weeks. Much of the content of these interviews centered around her frustration in attempting to communicate with her husband and her tolerance of what she felt to be his constant abuse. It was clear that this quiet, unassuming, apparently calm woman was deeply depressed about her current life situation. She felt empty and alone, rejected by her husband, and abandoned by her children. She gave no indication of anger.

Because her difficulties tended to be concentrated around the marital relationship, Ms. A and [the therapist] agreed that marital counseling was in order. She was dubious about her husband's potential compliance but prevailed on him to attend an initial interview. He quickly displayed the qualities his wife had ascribed to him. Mr. A, a short, round man who also appeared younger than his stated years, attacked his wife for not listening to him, accused her of infidelity and having a "mean temper," and gave her little opportunity to reply. He insisted that his wife agree with him because of his superior education and "understanding of psychology." He stressed to the therapist that his wife was "evil". . . , and he attributed these traits to her "going through the change of life." Ms. A offered little in reply except to state quietly and rather hopelessly that these charges were unfair.

Initially, the focus of the therapy was on providing an atmosphere in which Ms. A could tell her husband how his accusations made her feel. By the second session, she began to do this and, concurrently, to complain to Mr. A of the difficulties she had stated previously to me. This increased the tension in their relationship temporarily, but it also provided a more balanced conflict. The therapeutic focus could now shift to fostering awareness in each party of how his or her attacks made the other feel. Beginning with the fourth conjoint session, Mr. A acknowledged that his complaints about his wife made her feel bad. Ms. A grudgingly came to a similar awareness. . . . According to both parties, Mr. A reduced his attacks on his wife considerably after the fourth session.

After this session, Ms. A's blood pressure fell for the first time since her treatment at the clinic had begun. . . . There were no changes in medication or frequency of medical contacts. The marital [therapy] sessions were continued for four months, at which time Mr. A decided to discontinue the treatment, to his wife's displeasure. Ms. A continued [the therapy] on an individual basis for five more sessions. . . . Her blood pressure remained at the same level after termination of both individual and conjoint sessions.[14]

References for Further Reading

Note: Each of the following articles has a large number of references for reading in the various areas of the field of psychosomatics.

Frank, Jerome D., "Psychiatry, the Healthy Invalid," *American Journal of Psychiatry,* vol. 134, no. 12 (1977), pp. 1349-1355.

Lipowski, Z. J., "Psychosomatic Medicine in the Seventies: An Overview," *American Journal of Psychiatry,* vol. 134, no. 3 (1977), pp. 233-244.

Martin, M. J., "Psychosomatic Medicine: A Brief History," *Psychosomatics,* vol. 19, no. 11 (1978), pp. 697-700.

Sheehan, D., and Hackett, T., "Psychosomatic Disorders," in *Harvard Guide to Modern Psychiatry,* edited by Armand Nicholi. Cambridge: Harvard University Press, 1978.

 NINE

Psychotherapy

Throughout this book there have been many references to the form of treatment known as "psychotherapy." This chapter will present a more precise definition and fuller discussion of psychotherapy, and this information will aid the clergyperson in making more informed and appropriate referrals.

The Definition of Psychotherapy

Psychotherapy is a special form of human relationship, in which a person in some type of emotional distress (whom we shall call "the client") comes for help to a specially trained individual ("the psychotherapist"). The two individuals then go through a rather structured series of meetings in which the therapist tries to help the client to change his or her feelings, behaviors, or thoughts, and to regain a state of emotional health. In some forms of therapy the client is also helped to understand the root causes of the distress. (In this chapter, the term "therapist" always refers to psychotherapist, and "therapy" refers to psychotherapy.)

The psychotherapist works solely through verbal means—by listening, asking questions, and making comments and suggestions. While this may sound simple, it is not, for the therapist's comments and actions are thought out and based on a tested body of methods and theories. Furthermore, the therapist takes on a degree of responsibility for the outcome of the therapy and can be held ethically, or even legally, responsible for certain damages which might occur as a result of it.

Several other features are also characteristic of psychotherapy. The client and the therapist reach an agreement at the beginning of the process as to what they will do together and what their goals will be. In this agreement, the therapist is expected to represent his or her skills and training honestly and to stipulate what can and cannot be accomplished. The agreement is usually verbal and informal, but in some treatment settings it is actually written out and signed by both parties. Fees either are set by the therapist or are negotiated between therapist and client based on the client's income. The client agrees to pay for the services but has the freedom to withdraw at any time. The therapist agrees to utilize his or her skills in the service of the client and to continue until satisfactory goals are reached or until there is a mutual agreement to stop. If the therapist must withdraw unilaterally before the goals are reached, it is expected that he or she will arrange for the client to continue with another therapist.

The therapist also agrees to maintain confidentiality, a very important ingredient in the psychotherapy process. It is expected that, except for very unusual circumstances, the therapist will not reveal anything said or done by the client during the course of the therapy without the client's permission. It is only with this promise of confidentiality that psychotherapy can be effective.

Potentials and Limitations of Psychotherapy

It will be useful for the clergyperson to have some general idea of what psychotherapy can and cannot accomplish. Psychotherapy can bring about relief of psychological symptoms, such as anxiety, phobias, and mild depression, and relief of some physical symptoms as well. Beyond symptom relief, psychotherapy can lead to changes in some maladaptive personality traits, allowing the client to become more productive, more successful in interpersonal relationships, and generally happier with life. It can also help at least some individuals to become more aware of their feelings and more comfortable and appropriate in expressing those feelings. In marital and family therapy, the couple or family can be helped to have a deeper understanding of each other, to express needs and feelings more directly, and to settle conflicts more satisfactorily when they arise.

But it is probably more important to clarify what psychotherapy cannot do. Psychotherapy alone cannot relieve psychotic illnesses or severe depressions. When combined with medication, however, it can be quite helpful in these conditions. While therapy can change some personality traits, it cannot make an individual into a totally different person. It also cannot alleviate problems which are rooted in social or economic reality, such as the resentment and anger of the inner-city slum dweller who cannot find a job or pay the rent. Likewise, psychotherapy cannot take away the pain of major life traumas and grief reactions, although it can help people cope more effectively with these events.

Most important of all, psychotherapy cannot remove all conflicts and provide a state of constant happiness. Such a state might be attained by those who are willing to live in complete isolation. For the rest of the population, however, conflicts, struggles, and anxieties are an integral part of life, and psychotherapy can only help the client to meet these stresses more effectively and with less grief. Freud put it well in 1937 when he wrote about psychoanalysis:

> Our aim will not be to rub off every peculiarity of human character for the sake of a schematic "normality," nor yet to demand that the person who has been "thoroughly analysed" shall feel no passions and develop no internal conflicts. The business of the analysis is to secure the best possible psychological conditions for the functions of the ego; with that it has discharged its task.[1]

Types of Psychotherapy

In the past two decades, there has been an explosion on the clinical front, which at this writing is still continuing. The targets of psychotherapy have spread from individuals to families and groups, and then whole neighborhoods. Methods range from traditional interviews to tickling, nude marathons and elaborate rituals of meditation; practitioners have broken the bounds of the traditional disciplines and now include many whose only training is having undergone the therapy they offer to others, or who are simply fellow sufferers. The settings in which therapy is conducted have burst out of hospitals and offices to living rooms, motels and resorts. New psychotherapies spring up almost overnight. This lush overgrowth, of course, is in response to public demand, which seems insatiable. Persons are not only flocking to psychotherapies in droves, but are frantically searching for solutions to their personal problems in self-help books, which repeatedly make the best seller lists.[2]

This statement, written in 1978, sums up the current confusing state of affairs regarding different types of psychotherapy. Robert Harper, in his very useful small book, has collected thirty-six different systems of therapy;[3] no doubt there are even more by this time. One can sympathize with the clergyperson's confusion in trying to make an intelligent referral.

In the following section, we will briefly discuss the five types of psychotherapy which are probably most prevalent in this country. While they differ markedly in some ways, each is based on a well-thought-out body of theory and involves techniques which have been tested for at least twenty years.

Psychoanalysis

Psychoanalysis is a specific form of psychotherapy which was developed by Sigmund Freud and his followers in the early years of the twentieth century. It aims at uncovering root causes of emotional problems. These problems are thought to lie in childhood experiences and traumas.

In psychoanalysis, the client and the therapist (here known as the "analyst") meet very frequently—usually four or five hour-long sessions per week. The client lies on a couch and cannot see the analyst. This arrangement is designed to make the client completely comfortable and free of distractions during the hour. The client is encouraged to voice whatever thoughts come to mind, no matter how irrelevant they may seem at the time. The analyst allows the client to determine what is talked about and to set the pace of the therapy, and makes relatively few comments during the process. Psychoanalysts believe that if the client is allowed to follow the lead of his or her spontaneous thoughts and feelings, the roots of the client's emotional difficulties will eventually be revealed. This rambling process, however, takes a good deal of time, and it is not unusual for an analysis to continue for four or five years.

Psychoanalysis is a very rich emotional experience for the client. The unstructured analytic situation brings out a wealth of feelings and memories and allows a great deal of time for these to be discussed and understood. But psychoanalysis is obviously not the treatment of choice for everyone. From a very practical point of view, few people can afford the tremendous outlay of money and time which the process requires. Furthermore, the analytic client must be fairly healthy to begin with, since he or she is expected to take a great deal of initiative in the therapy and to persevere for a very long period of time despite the many painful hours which are involved.

Freud himself never claimed that analysis was a treatment for everyone; in fact, he believed that it was primarily a research method which could uncover the deepest levels of the unconscious for scientific study. It was Freud's later followers who attempted to apply it very widely as a treatment technique, and in the 1930s and 1940s it was presented as the answer to virtually all emotional problems. In the last thirty years, however, we have come to realize that psychoanalysis is a method suitable for only a very small proportion of the population—those people who are nonpsychotic, intelligent, articulate, highly motivated, and possessing the requisite resources of time and money. For a person with these characteristics, analysis can be an extremely rewarding and growth-producing experience.[4]

The contributions of psychoanalysis should not be minimized, even though it is suitable for only a small number of people. These relatively few analytic clients continue to provide the rest of the mental health field with a wealth of insights into the unconscious. Furthermore, psychoanalysis gave rise to the next form of therapy to be discussed, which is much more widely used and has benefited large numbers of people.

Analytic-Oriented Psychotherapy

In the 1940s a number of psychoanalysts began developing a new form of psychotherapy which was based on the theories of psychoanalysis but was briefer and more flexible in its techniques. In this newer method—which came to be known as "analytic-oriented therapy"—the therapist is much more active than in psychoanalysis and takes more of a part in directing the flow of conversation. The client sits up, facing the therapist; sessions are held once or twice a week; and the average duration of treatment is one to three years. The aim of the therapy, like analysis, is to uncover underlying causes of present emotional difficulties and to show how the past is played out in the client's present life. Some of the emotional richness and depth of psychoanalysis is lost in this therapy, but the overall process is greatly streamlined.

Because it does not require such great amounts of time, money, and initiative, analytic-oriented psychotherapy is applicable to many more people than is psychoanalysis. A large proportion of the psychotherapy done in the United States falls into this category.

Behavior Therapy

Until the 1950s psychoanalysis and analytic-oriented therapy dominated the psychotherapy field in the United States. The first major departure from this tradition came about with the development of behavior therapy, a method of treatment based on an entirely different set of theories. This school of therapists conceptualizes emotional problems in terms of learning and behavior. They argue that faulty behavior patterns, learned early in life, are the key cause of emotional difficulties. If these behavior patterns can be changed, they believe that the associated emotional problems will be resolved as a consequence of the behavior change.

In behavioral psychotherapy, there is very little attempt made to recover childhood memories or get to ''root causes'' in the past. Instead, the therapist uses special techniques to change certain specific patterns of the client's behavior. The particular patterns are chosen by the therapist and the client during the early therapy sessions. The therapist is quite active and actually instructs the client in the techniques, and the client is expected to practice the techniques and do ''homework'' between the weekly sessions. Duration of treatment is usually relatively short (six to twelve months).

Behavior therapy is most effective for those individuals who are suffering from limited psychological symptoms or difficulties, but who have basically well-functioning personalities. Such problems include phobias, ritualistic habits, or difficulties of assertiveness in specific situations.[5]

Gestalt Therapy

Gestalt psychotherapy is based on a theory which stresses the idea that healthy individuals experience themselves, their past, and the world around them in configurations or patterns (*Gestalten* in German). These configurations involve a rich interplay of ideas, feelings, and physical sensations. The emotionally troubled person, according to this theory, has suffered a fragmentation of this process of gestalt formation; aspects of this person's experience and memory have become blocked off from conscious awareness but continue to create problems for the individual. The Gestalt therapist believes that these blocked-off feelings, memories, and sensations can be made conscious by vigorous therapeutic interventions and specific techniques. The client is then able to understand himself or herself more clearly and to act in more productive ways.

In practice, Gestalt therapy is an emotionally intense experience in which the therapist is quite active and confronting. In addition to discussion, dramatic techniques are used, and the client is often encouraged to "act out" painful feelings and experiences. As this is done, the therapist intervenes to change the experience. For example, a client who lost his father at an early age through a sudden death might be encouraged to have an imaginary conversation with his father, voicing all of the feelings which had never been expressed in real life. The client might also be instructed to play the role of the father, giving the latter's imagined responses to the son.

As one can see, Gestalt therapy requires that the client be both imaginative and able to withstand much direct confrontation and emotional catharsis. The duration of therapy is short, and therapy is sometimes done in extended sessions in a group setting.

In the United States, the undisputed master of Gestalt therapy was Dr. Fritz Perls, who died in 1970. The clearest picture of Gestalt therapy in action can be found in the transcripts in his book *Gestalt Therapy Verbatim*.[6]

Transactional Analysis

This school of psychotherapy was founded by Dr. Eric Berne, whose well-known book *Games People Play*[7] appeared in 1964. In the theory of Transactional Analysis (T.A.), it is believed that each person's life is lived according to a set of rules—called, in T.A. terms, a "script"—which is laid down in early childhood and then becomes unconscious, although its effects continue to be evident throughout life. Under the influence of the "script," an individual interacts with other people by following certain patterns of behavior, called "games," each of which has its own "rules" and "payoffs" for the winner.

Each person is also thought of as having three different aspects, or "ego-states"—a harsh, critical aspect (the "parent"); an impulsive, pleasure-seeking, irrational aspect (the "child"); and an objective, sensible, mature aspect (the "adult"). When the "child" aspect of the individual is dominant, the "script" is played out unconsciously, outside of the person's awareness, resulting in many "games" which end up being nonproductive, painful, or even destructive.

T.A. therapy aims at strengthening the "adult" aspect of the person, making the "script" and the "games" conscious, and changing them. Techniques are limited to discussion and often resemble those of analytic-oriented therapy, with meetings once or twice a week, a fairly active therapist, and an average duration of therapy of one to two years.

Eclectic Psychotherapy

Five different types of psychotherapy have been described above, but in practice many therapists do not confine themselves exclusively to any one type. Instead, they do what is called "eclectic" therapy—they choose and combine techniques and theories from two or more schools. These therapists are familiar with several different approaches and can vary their techniques according to the client's personality and the nature of the problem being treated. A therapist usually has one primary orientation, with other approaches being used secondarily. The therapist's ability to use different approaches adds greatly to richness of the therapy experience and the variety of clients who can be helped.

Modalities of Therapy

Psychotherapy can also be classified according to the number of clients who are treated in the sessions. In *individual therapy,* one client is seen by one therapist; in *marital therapy,* a married couple is seen jointly and treated together by one therapist. *Family therapy* is the treatment of an entire family: all family members are present at each session, and there may be either one or two therapists. *Group therapy* involves the treatment of a group of clients—usually between five and ten—by either one or two therapists. In each of these modalities, the therapist may use any of the theoretical approaches described above, or an eclectic approach which combines elements of several schools of thought.

Things to Know About Psychotherapy

The clergyperson may be in an ideal position to refer a good number of people for psychotherapy and to support them as they go through the therapeutic process. In order to do this effectively, it is important that he or she understand certain basic features of psychotherapy.

Psychotherapy must be voluntary.

Psychotherapy is a method of treatment which is effective only when the client accepts help voluntarily. A person who is sentenced to psychotherapy by the court or forced into it by family pressure is not likely to gain much benefit from it. As will be discussed below, the process of psychotherapy requires that the client be an active, willing participant, not a passive and grudging recipient.

The clergyperson can certainly recommend psychotherapy and can even urge an individual to pursue it, but should never attempt to force it on the individual, and should dissuade others from using such coercion. The most fruitful way to make a referral for psychotherapy is to plant the suggestion in the individual's mind and then allow time for the idea and the motivation to develop. Tact and restraint are essential. It may take days or weeks for the individual to make the voluntary decision to seek therapy, but the chances of a successful outcome will be much greater once this free choice is made.

This factor is particularly important when the client is an adolescent who is involved in conflicts with parents. It is relatively easy for parents to force a teenage child to go to a therapist and to pay the bill for the services. But the adolescent, like the proverbial horse, can only be led to the water; he or she cannot be forced to "drink" unless there is an independent desire to do so.

Because of these considerations, most therapists will not begin therapy unless there is some indication of motivation on the part of the client, apart from any pressures from family, friends, spouse, clergy, etc. In fact, many therapists will not even make an initial appointment unless the client has enough interest to make a personal contact. The practical reason for this is that in the great majority of these "third party'' appointments, the client simply fails to show up. If the client is realistically so impaired as to be unable to function independently, the therapist will usually recommend another form of treatment.

In psychotherapy, the client is not told what to do.

In the traditional model of medical treatment, the patient first describes to the doctor the symptoms which are present and gives other specific information in response to the doctor's questions. The physician then takes over, doing an examination and dispensing the treatment. In this second phase of the process, the patient is a more or less passive recipient who follows the doctor's directions. It is assumed that the patient is relatively ignorant regarding the illness and the treatment and that the doctor is the expert who knows what is best for the patient.

Many people come to psychotherapy expecting that it will be like the medical model described above—the therapist will tell them what to do and their role will be to follow directions. These people are often confused and disappointed to find that this is not the case.

Psychotherapy is a cooperative venture of two or more individuals working together. The therapist does not tell the client what to do; he or she may make suggestions and will certainly point out new aspects of the problems, but decisions as to courses of action are always up to the client. Even in behavior therapy, which is perhaps the most directive of all the psychotherapies, the client is expected to make the basic decision of defining the goals and behaviors to be worked on. The therapist does not know beforehand what is ''best'' for the client but instead helps the client discover what is best for that individual. The uniqueness of the psychotherapy situation is that it allows the client to test out a number of options, both in thought and in action, with a therapist who will neither reject nor criticize.

This does not mean, however, that a therapist will condone *any* behavior on the part of the client; every therapist has his or her limits beyond which a neutral accepting stance is no longer possible. Acts which are illegal or grossly dangerous will usually be so labeled by the therapist, and if the client persists in such acts, the therapy may have to be terminated.

Mr. L had a history of assaultive behavior and depression and had been in psychotherapy for two months. During one session, in response to a comment by the therapist, he became enraged and threw an ashtray across the office, narrowly missing the therapist's head. The therapist responded by telling Mr. L directly that the therapy could not continue if behavior such as this was repeated. He stated that he was willing to talk with Mr. L about any feelings that he was having, but that he could not allow Mr. L to act on those feelings in a destructive manner.

Mr. Q started therapy because of difficulties in relationships with women and periodic depressions. After about four months in therapy, he revealed a pattern of behavior which had been occurring for about three years. Mr. Q stated that from time to time he had had sexual relations with animals on a farm which was near his home.

The therapist listened to the account and asked some questions to clarify the facts. He then said that he intended to keep this information confidential, like everything else Mr. Q had told him. He added, however, that it was his duty to point out to Mr. Q that what he was doing carried serious consequences if he were to be discovered. These consequences included adverse publicity, public embarrassment, and even legal action, since what he was doing was considered a criminal offense. The therapist also remarked that he wondered why Mr. Q would take such chances with his future, and invited Mr. Q to think about this question. He urged Mr. Q to talk about this behavior, and the feelings that accompanied it, instead of actually carrying it out.

Psychotherapy requires the client's active participation.

In psychotherapy, unlike the usual medical situation, the causes of the client's problems or symptoms cannot be discovered by physical examination or laboratory studies but only by an ongoing process of investigation of the client's present life and past background. The therapist needs the client at every step of this process to supply information about events, thoughts, and feelings. Therapists do not have the ability to read minds or to see the past or future in a crystal ball. The therapist can help the client to understand the "data" of his or her life in a new way and thereby make changes in feelings and behavior—but the data itself must be supplied by the client.

The clergyperson can be extremely helpful to an individual who is beginning psychotherapy by helping the individual in the process of readjustment of expectations.

Psychotherapy takes time to complete.

Patterns of thinking and behavior are built up slowly over the course of many years of life experience. Much of this "patterning" occurs during childhood, when the growing child is not even aware of the process which is taking place and is unable to separate maladaptive traits from those which are healthy and fulfilling. By the time an individual reaches the point of wanting to change these patterns, they are usually quite fixed, and the process of change is of necessity not easy.

Because of this, psychotherapy takes time. A very small number of people may be flexible enough to make significant changes after only a few sessions, but for the majority, the process must be more prolonged. At least several months are required, and possibly as long as two or three years.

The length of therapy in each case must be determined by the therapist, based on the client's needs and the nature of the problems; financial considerations may also play a part in this determination. Therapists as a rule try to be flexible about setting the length of treatment, and the plan may change during the treatment. New problems may be revealed which require additional time; conversely, the client may prove to be more amenable to change than was apparent at first, and progress may be surprisingly rapid. Both the therapist and the client should avoid becoming "locked in" to a particular timetable but should be prepared to renegotiate whenever necessary.

It is reasonable, however, for the client to expect to be told at the first visit the therapist's best estimate of the length of therapy. If this information is not offered spontaneously by the therapist, the client should feel free to ask for it directly. A certain degree of ambiguity is an essential part of psychotherapy, but there is no reason for a client to come away from a first therapy session with no idea whatever as to the length of the treatment which lies ahead.

During the therapy itself, patience is an essential ingredient for ultimate success. The client should understand that immediate "solutions" may have to be postponed, but it is hoped that the ultimate result will justify the discomfort. He or she should be encouraged to continue the therapy, even during those periods when nothing seems to be happening.

Occasionally it may happen that an extended period of therapy—six months or more—may pass without any improvement in problems, or with worsening of those problems. In a case such as this, the client may turn to the clergyperson for advice. The most appropriate course of action in this instance is not for the client to leave therapy. It is also not advisable—for reasons which will be discussed later—for the clergyperson to intervene on the client's behalf, even if the client requests this. The client should instead be counseled to speak openly and frankly to the therapist, voicing whatever questions and dissatisfactions are present. The client may be reluctant to do this, but it is crucial that it be done, and the clergyperson's encouragement can be a very important factor here. A frank discussion between therapist and client usually can bring about a satisfactory resolution to the problem and may be a growth-producing experience for the client. In the extreme case, where all discussion between client and therapist has failed to satisfy the client, an outside consultation with another therapist may be obtained. The arrangements for such a consultation, if it becomes necessary, should be made openly and jointly by the therapist and the client.

The reasons for the clergyperson's not intervening directly in such a situation are twofold. First, the rule of confidentiality will probably prevent the therapist from discussing details of the therapy with any third party, including clergy. Even if this obstacle can be avoided, a second and greater problem remains. Psychotherapy, by its very nature, attempts to foster independence and personal initiative, rather than passivity and overreliance on others. To put it in other terms, psychotherapy encourages the client to act as much as possible as a self-sufficient adult, rather than as a child who needs others to act in his or her behalf. The clergyperson who volunteers or agrees to intervene for the client is unwittingly treating the client as though he or she were too weak or immature to act independently. This undermines one of the key efforts of psychotherapy and can become a self-fulfilling prophecy: a person who is treated like a child often continues to act like one.

This is a difficult point because it may appear to go against the clergyperson's natural desire to be helpful. But there is another way to view this process: by gently insisting on the client's self-sufficiency and maturity, the clergyperson is actually being helpful in a much deeper and longer-lasting way.

Psychotherapy requires confidentiality and discourages third parties.

As noted above, confidentiality is one of the keystones of the therapeutic process and is absolutely necessary if the client is to feel comfortable enough to share very personal feelings. The clergyperson will understand, therefore, why therapists do not give out information, even to the client's immediate family, without the client's full knowledge and consent. Furthermore, most therapists will not accept information about clients from a third party unless the client is aware of that information.

> John R., a twenty-one-year-old college dropout, was living at home with his parents and was in therapy with Dr. W. One day, Mrs. R, John's mother, called Dr. W. She said she was very concerned about John's recent behavior and wanted to make sure that Dr. W knew what was happening; however, she did not want John to know that she had called. She stated that she was afraid John would be angry at her for calling, and that this would damage their relationship, which was already a difficult one.
>
> Dr. W replied that he appreciated her concern and would be glad to hear whatever she wanted to tell him. He added, however, that no secrets could be kept and that John would be told about the call.
>
> At first Mrs. R was angry and exclaimed that Dr. W was being unreasonable. The therapist explained that there were several reasons for his position. First of all, he had made an agreement with John that they would always be as open as possible with each other and not conceal information: he expected John to keep his end of the bargain, and therefore had to uphold his own as well. Secondly, he pointed out that Mrs. R had said in a previous interview that she wanted John to "grow up," yet in this instance was treating him like a child by hiding information from him. Finally, he remarked that it would probably be good for John to know that his mother was concerned, and it might actually strengthen their relationship.

After a pause, Mrs. R replied that she could see Dr. W's point. The therapist then suggested that instead of telling him the information, she go directly to John and talk openly with him about her concerns. John could then discuss the problems with Dr. W at the next therapy session.

This example is presented in some detail to give the reader an idea of a therapist's motivation in the handling of a delicate situation. The therapist who refuses to break confidentiality or to keep secrets is not acting out of stubbornness or out of a desire to punish the family, but is defending a fundamental aspect of the psychotherapy contract.

The reader may see a similarity between this example and the discussion in the previous section. Psychotherapy encourages open, direct communication between individuals and discourages the intervention of all third parties whenever possible. In the previous discussion, the clergyperson was advised not to be enticed into a situation which rightfully involves only the client and the therapist. In this case, the therapist himself was being drawn in as a third party to an issue that should have been handled directly between Mrs. R and her son, and he resisted being used in this manner.

Psychotherapy is not always pleasant.

During the course of psychotherapy it is often necessary for the client to revive unhappy memories and experience painful feelings. This is considered, in most forms of therapy, to be essential to the process of recovery and growth. It is believed that the repression of these feelings creates or aggravates many forms of emotional illness.

Bringing unpleasant feelings to the surface, however, is not an easy matter. In order to function from day to day, each person learns quite early in life to keep such feelings out of awareness, and these mechanisms of suppression can be extremely strong. Even those individuals who are sincerely motivated for change will therefore resist the therapist's attempts to bring out negative feelings. This resistance can take many forms, ranging from simple refusal to talk about certain subjects to missing appointments or terminating therapy altogether. To gain maximum benefit from therapy, the client must fight against his or her own resistance and persist in the effort despite painful moments. The therapist will certainly help in this undertaking, but the client's effort is indispensable in following the therapy to its conclusion.

The psychotherapy situation is set up in such a way to facilitate the expression of negative feelings. Confidentiality is assured, and the usual rules of "polite" conversation are suspended. It is expected that the client and therapist will treat each other with decency and respect, but it is also understood that any thoughts or feelings, no matter how unpleasant, aberrant, or socially unacceptable, can be discussed. The therapist accepts whatever feelings the client voices, without condemnation.

These rules apply even to unpleasant feelings which the client has about the therapist. These are not only accepted but also are considered particularly important for discussion. An individual who is in psychotherapy should be encouraged to express whatever feelings he or she is experiencing directly to the therapist.

In marital therapy, the primary object is not always to preserve the marriage.

Married couples who are having difficulties in their relationships are often referred by clergy to clinics or private practitioners for marital therapy. Such a referral is quite appropriate, but the clergyperson should have a basic understanding of the aims of marital therapy, so as not to hold false expectations or convey them to the couple being referred.

In marital psychotherapy, the therapist attempts to help both members of the couple to widen their understanding of themselves and of each other. The therapist helps the partners to identify and elucidate the problems which exist in their relationship and guides them as they find solutions to those problems. The aim of marital therapy is to find solutions which are as constructive and growth producing as possible for both partners, and for the children of those partners as well.

In a general sense, all marital therapists would probably agree that marriages should be preserved wherever possible. The skyrocketing rate of divorce in our society is a source of concern for all mental health professionals. On the other hand, however, there are some marriages which are so full of conflict and unhappiness that separation and divorce are the most humane solutions for all concerned. It has been demonstrated through repeated experience that keeping two very discontented partners together "for the sake of the children" often succeeds in scarring the children—and the parents—even more deeply.

For this reason, marital therapists usually make it clear to their clients at the outset that they are dedicated neither to the preservation of marriages nor to their destruction, but rather to helping each couple find its own unique solutions to its problems. If, after extended discussion and consideration, it seems to the couple that divorce is the best course to follow, the therapist will help the partners to accomplish that process as smoothly and maturely as possible.

Choosing a Therapist

Psychotherapy is practiced by many different professionals, with many different backgrounds and training. A few states have instituted procedures for examination and licensing of all psychotherapists, but the majority of states have not. In most parts of this country, therefore, it is fairly easy for an individual to represent himself or herself publicly as a "psychotherapist," even without very much in the way of professional credentials. How then should the clergyperson go about selecting a therapist for a parishioner who seems to need this type of help?

First of all, it is assumed that the individual being referred does not fall into one of the five categories discussed in previous chapters: the psychotic, the suicidal, the severely depressed, the drug or alcohol abuser, or the person with organic brain disease. These five types of individuals should always be referred to a psychiatrist, a psychiatric facility, or a Community Mental Health Center.

For individuals outside these five categories, the clergyperson has a broader range of referral options. If the clergyperson is unfamiliar with the practitioners in the community, it is probably safest to refer to an institution, such as pastoral counseling center or a mental health clinic. One can usually assume that the institution has ensured that only competent persons are on its staff and that the client will be matched with the most appropriate therapist. The clergyperson can also be guided by the reputation of the institution in the community.

Selecting a private-practice psychotherapist is not as easy, for here the clergyperson must make some judgments, both as to the practitioner's qualifications and as to the quality of the match between the therapist and the client being referred. As stated in chapter 2, the best approach is one of honesty and frankness. The clergyperson should first find out about the therapist's educational background. A psychotherapist should always have some advanced training beyond the bachelor's degree level; that training should be either in a professional school (medical school, graduate department of psychology, or school of social work) or in a specific training program for psychotherapy.

As a further measure of competence, one may ask whether the therapist is a member of a professional association in his or her field. A partial list of these associations is given in Table 1. Each of these associations requires that its members meet certain standards of training, experience, and ongoing education.

Table 1
Some Professional Organizations in Which Psychotherapists May Have Membership

American Psychiatric Association
American Psychological Association
National Association of Social Workers
American Association of Marriage and Family Therapists
American Association of Pastoral Counselors
American Orthopsychiatric Association
American Academy of Child Psychiatry
American Group Psychotherapy Association
International Transactional Analysis Association

In assessing the therapist's qualifications, the clergyperson may also wish to inquire as to years of experience, but this information must be interpreted carefully. A young therapist with good credentials and a solid professional manner should not be discounted because of relative lack of experience. By the same token, many years of practice do not necessarily imply excellence.

Beyond these objective measures of qualification, the clergyperson should also assess the therapist's general bearing and behavior. A therapist should ideally project a sense of confidence and of knowing what to do, yet do so without abrasiveness or arrogance. These qualities are measured by subjective standards which are not precise, but are nonetheless very important. The client must have a good personal rapport with the therapist and must have a basically positive feeling about their relationship. Without this rapport, the therapy will be very difficult or even impossible, despite the therapist's training and background.

The clergyperson should also inquire as to the therapist's theoretical orientation and the type of therapy which he or she does. Each of the different types of therapy described earlier in this chapter is suited to a different type of personality or problem. Behavior therapy, for example, with its concrete, action-oriented techniques, appeals to a very different group of people than does psychoanalysis or analytic-oriented therapy.

Ideally, the clergyperson should be acquainted with several different practitioners, with different orientations and personality styles. With experience, the clergyperson can become a successful "matchmaker" between therapists and clients.

References for Further Reading

Meissner, W., and Nicholi, Armand, "The Psychotherapies," in *Harvard Guide to Modern Psychiatry*, edited by Armand Nicholi. Cambridge: Harvard University Press, 1978.

Frank, Jerome D., *Persuasion and Healing: A Comparative Study of Psychotherapy*. Baltimore: The Johns Hopkins University Press, 1973. (Paperback: Schocken)

Loew, Clemens A.; Grayson, H.; and Loew G., eds., *Three Psychotherapies*. New York: Brunner/Mazel, Inc., 1975.

Notes

Chapter 1

[1] Gerald Gurin, Joseph Veroff, and Sheila Feld, *Americans View Their Mental Health* (New York: Basic Books, Inc., 1960).

[2] Joseph Veroff, Elizabeth Douvan, and R. Kulka, *Americans View Their Mental Health* (Ann Arbor: Survey Research Center, University of Michigan, 1976).

[3] *Report of the President's Commission on Mental Health* (Washington: U. S. Government Printing Office, 1978), vol. 2, p. 192.

Chapter 4

[1] Roger A. MacKinnon and Robert Michels, *The Psychiatric Interview in Clinical Practice* (Philadelphia: W. B. Saunders Company, 1971), p. 206.

[2] "Principles of Medical Ethics with Annotations Especially Applicable to Psychiatry," *American Journal of Psychiatry*, vol. 130, no. 9 (1973), pp. 1058-1064; see especially p. 1059.

Chapter 5

[1] Maria Kovacs and Aaron T. Beck, "Maladaptive Cognitive Structures in Depression," *American Journal of Psychiatry*, vol. 135 (1978), pp. 525-533.

[2] Erich Lindemann, "Symptomatology and Management of Acute Grief," *American Journal of Psychiatry*, vol. 101 (1944), pp. 141-148.

[3] William W. K. Zung, "A Self-Rating Depression Scale," *Archives of General Psychiatry*, vol. 12 (1965), pp. 63-70. Copyright © 1965, American Medical Association.

[4] For a firsthand description of the experience of severe depression and its treatment

153

in the 1920s, see the chapter entitled "A Season in Hell," in Van Wyck Brooks's autobiography, *Days of the Phoenix* (New York: E. P. Dutton & Company, Inc., 1957), pp. 183-193.

Chapter 6

[1]For an interesting experimental study of social roles among drinking alcoholics, see Peter Steinglass and Sheldon Weiner, "Familial Interactions and Determinants of Drinking Behavior" in Nancy K. Mello and Jack H. Mendelson, eds., *Recent Advances in Studies of Alcoholism* (Rockville, Md.: National Institutes of Mental Health, 1971), pp. 687-704.

[2]John Schwartzman, "The Addict, Abstinence, and the Family," *American Journal of Psychiatry,* vol. 132 (1975), p. 156. This article has twenty-one references and will serve as a good starting point for further reading on this subject.

[3]Eric Berne, *Games People Play* (New York: Grove Press, Inc., 1964), pp. 73-81.

[4]Claude Steiner, *Games Alcoholics Play* (New York: Grove Press, Inc., 1971).

[5]A.A. is one of the best known and most successful treatment programs for substance abuse. For a full description and analysis of this organization, see Margaret Bean, "Alcoholics Anonymous," *Psychiatric Annals,* vol. 5, no. 2 (1975), pp. 45-61; vol. 5, no. 3 (1975), pp. 83-109.

Chapter 7

[1]J. Ronald D. Bayne, "Assessing Confusion in the Elderly," *Psychosomatics,* vol. 20, no. 1 (1979), pp. 43-51.

Chapter 8

[1]Sigmund Freud, *Studies on Hysteria,* The Standard Edition of the Complete Psychological Works of Sigmund Freud, vol. 2 (London: The Hogarth Press, 1955).

[2]Franz Alexander et al., *Studies in Psychosomatic Medicine* (New York: The Ronald Press Company, 1948); and Franz Alexander, *Psychosomatic Medicine* (New York: W. W. Norton & Co., Inc., 1950).

[3]Alexander, *Psychosomatic Medicine,* pp. 204-205.

[4]*Ibid.,* pp. 180-181.

[5]Marvin Stein, Raul C. Schiavi, and Maria Camerino, "Influence of Brain and Behavior on the Immune System," *Science,* vol. 191 (1976), pp. 435-440.

[6]J. B. Imboden, "Psychosocial Determinants of Recovery," *Advances in Psychosomatic Medicine,* vol. 8 (1972), pp. 142-155.

[7]Randall C. Mason, Jr.; Graham Clark; Robert B. Reeves, Jr., et al., "Acceptance and Healing," *Journal of Religion and Health,* vol. 8 (1969), p. 140.

[8]William A. Greene, Jr., "Psychological Factors and Reticuloendothelial Disease" (Part I), *Psychosomatic Medicine,* vol. 16 (1954), pp. 220-230; and William A. Greene, Lawrence E. Young, and Scott N. Swisher, "Psychological Factors and Reticuloendothelial Disease," *Psychosomatic Medicine,* vol. 18 (1956), pp. 284-303. Reprinted by permission of publisher. Copyright 1954 and 1956 by Elsevier North Holland, Inc.

[9]Greene (1954), *op. cit.,* p. 226.

[10]*Ibid.*

[11]Greene et al. (1956), *op cit.,* p. 299.

[12]For a review of a number of these studies, see Constance Holden, "Cancer and the Mind," *Science,* vol. 200 (1978), pp. 1363-1369.

[13]P. E. Sifneos, "The Prevalence of 'Alexithymic' Characteristics in Psychosomatic Patients," *Psychotherapy and Psychosomatics,* vol. 22 (1973), pp. 255-262; and I. Lesser, C. Ford, and C. Friedman, "Alexithymia in Somatizing Patients," *General*

Hospital Psychiatry, vol. 1 (1979), pp. 256-261.

¹⁴Frank Summers, "Severe Hypertension Treated Successfully by Marital Psycho-therapy," *American Journal of Psychiatry,* vol. 135 (1978), p. 989.

Chapter 9

¹Sigmund Freud, "Analysis Terminable and Interminable," in The Standard Edition of the Complete Psychological Works of Sigmund Freud (London: The Hogarth Press, 1953), vol. 23, p. 250.

²Jerome D. Frank, Rudolph Hoehn-Saric, Stanley Imber et al., *Effective Ingredients of Successful Psychotherapy* (New York: Brunner/Mazel, Inc., 1978), pp. xi-xii.

³Robert A. Harper, *Psychoanalysis and Psychotherapy: 36 Systems* (New York: Jason Aronson, Inc., 1974).

⁴For a well-written lay person's introduction to psychoanalysis, see Calvin Springer Hall, *A Primer of Freudian Psychology* (New York: New American Library, 1954).

⁵For a general overview of behavior therapy, see A. Robert Sherman, *Behavior Modification: Theory and Practice* (Belmont, Calif.: Wadsworth Publishing Co., 1973), also paperback by Brooks/Cole Publishing Co.

⁶Frederick S. Perls, *Gestalt Therapy Verbatim* (Moab, Utah: Real People Press, 1969), also paperback by Bantam.

⁷Eric Berne, *Games People Play* (New York: Grove Press, Inc., 1964); see also C. Steiner, *Scripts People Live* (New York: Grove Press, Inc., 1974).

Index